Quarterly Essay

CONTENTS

Quarterly Essay is published four times a year by Black Inc., an imprint of Schwartz Publishing Pty Ltd
Publisher: Morry Schwartz

ISBN 186 395 1652

Subscriptions (4 issues): $49 a year within Australia incl. GST (Institutional subs. $59). Outside Australia $79. Payment may be made by Mastercard, Visa or Bankcard, or by cheque made out to Schwartz Publishing. Payment includes postage and handling.

To subscribe, fill out and post the subscription form on the last page of this essay, or subscribe online at:

www.quarterlyessay.com

Correspondence and subscriptions should be addressed to the Editor at:
Black Inc.
Level 5, 289 Flinders Lane
Melbourne VIC 3000 Australia
Phone: 61 3 9654 2000
Fax: 61 3 9654 2290
Email: quarterlyessay@blackincbooks.com
http://www.quarterlyessay.com

Editor: Chris Feik
Management: Sophy Williams
Editorial Co-ordinator: Caitlin Yates
Publicity: Meredith Kelly
Design: Guy Mirabella

INTRODUCTION

I had been going to Baghdad for fifteen years before I had the fifteen-minute conversation that alerted me to the extraordinary power of the tribes of Iraq. At a private dinner in Jordan, in the aftermath of the US-led invasion, Arab friends urged me to research the role of the tribes. I trusted their judgement, so I did.

I have been to Iraq four times in just over a year – usually for eight to ten weeks at a time, and usually camping at the Palestine Hotel, on the eastern bank of the Tigris River, where this essay started coming together as I wrote my reports for *The Sydney Morning Herald* and *The Age*. Whatever angle of the Iraq story I was pursuing on a given day, I'd also have my fixers and translators guide me deeper into the exotic world of the tribes and the mosques.

For most of the last decade, it was the power of Saddam Hussein that transfixed reporters going to Iraq, and it was only when they were released from his iron grip that Iraqis could provide outsiders with an unvarnished portrait of forces that had been suppressed for decades. Iraqis call their men of power *sheikhs*. In the tribes, fathers hand to their sons power over the lives of their people; in the mosques, many of the sheikhs take their authority from a born-to-rule blood-line that goes all the way back to Mohammed. The more I saw of the sheikhs, and the more I talked with them, the more clearly I realised that the most fundamental power structures in Iraqi society run counter to those which underpin democracy.

When Westerners look at the Middle East, many mistakenly see a region of countries. But those national borders are a Western imposition; in reality, it's a region of tribes and religions. It is essential to understand this if we are to hazard a guess at the outcome of the latest Western intervention in a part of the world that has stubbornly resisted democracy for all of its history.

I had hardly caught my breath at the military success of the US-led invasion when it began to emerge, rapidly and violently, that the occupation of Iraq could be a failure. What the US bills as "freedom" is seen by too many Iraqis as "occupation". My Jordanian friends had said as much – if the Americans did not have the support of the tribes, they would fail. Equally, the occupation was unlikely to deliver Washington's democratic beachhead in the Middle East unless it had the support of the Shiite spiritual leadership.

Before the war, the US failed to support the tribes' attempts to overthrow Saddam. Iraqi history would have unfolded very differently had any of the coup attempts succeeded; instead, the US set itself on a collision course with the tribes. Today there is a vacuum where legitimate authority should be, and all of Iraq's conflicts are expanding to fill it. Perhaps, then, this is a story of hubris. The US did not allow leading Iraqi voices a say in Iraq's future. That, you'd have to say, is a peculiar way to bring democracy to a sceptical nation.

There'll be arguments that it's politically incorrect, racist even, to question the ability or desire of Arabs to embrace democracy. Nevertheless, if governments in the United States, Britain and Australia have staked their future on a presumption that the Middle East can be democratised, it's necessary to grasp what they seem to have misunderstood. Instead of exploring political theory and comparative sociology, I have sought to allow Iraqi voices to reveal why today's Iraq is not the nursery for democracy that Washington wants it to be.

This *Quarterly Essay* would not have been possible without the enthusiastic backing of John Fairfax Publications, publishers of *The Sydney Morning Herald* and *The Age*. In particular, I thank Robert Whitehead, editor of the *Herald*, for his support.

Paul McGeough

MISSION IMPOSSIBLE

The Sheikhs, the US and the Future of Iraq

Paul McGeough

The country beyond Ramadi flattens out like a cracker biscuit. A six-lane desert highway stretches westward, all the way to Jordan. At times it crosses ribbons of green, sketching the route of irrigation canals; in other places it detours around the scenes of battle – charred tanks and trucks, broken bridges and decapitated date palms.

Before the war, the GMC four-wheel-drive would head north for a couple of miles, taking a sandy track over the railroad and away from "the big house". When it paused briefly at a junction near the eighteen-kilometre marker on the Jordan highway, the tribal sheikh behind the wheel was taking his life into his hands. Literally. If Malik Abdul Karim al-Kharbit turned left, he was going to Amman. It meant that as one of the more powerful tribal leaders in all of Iraq, he was putting his family and his business empire on the line. He was headed for the Jordanian capital, about 800 kilometres away, where he would betray Saddam Hussein in secret meetings with United States intelligence agents. Under the cover of social engagements with senior government officials and sometimes with the King of Jordan himself, Sheikh Malik regularly delivered price-less information that had been fed to him by members of his Kharbit clan and by others who held positions at all levels of Hussein's military and security apparatus. An official who attended some of these debriefings was emphatic: "Malik was very much Washington's man in Iraq." Now Sheikh Malik is dead, but it wasn't Saddam Hussein who killed him – it was the Americans.

In the avalanche of reporting that marked the collapse of Baghdad early in April 2003, little attention was paid to a one-line statement from the US Central Command, a claim that the US had bombed the home of Barzan Ibrahim Hasan al-Tikriti, a half-brother to Saddam Hussein, who at one stage had been head of Iraqi intelligence. The attack was on 11 April, only two days after the demolition of the great Saddam statue in central Baghdad. Reporters were told that six JDAM smart bombs had hammered into a house near Ramadi, in the centre of Iraq. There was brief speculation that Barzan was dead – that a joker had gone from the Americans' "most-wanted" deck of cards. But when CENTCOM announced six days later that, in fact, Barzan was alive and had just been captured in the capital, no questions were asked and the story just moved right on. Barzan did have a stake in a poultry farm about five kilo-metres west of Ramadi, which locals said had been bombed by the US on 4 April, but he was not known to have a residence in the area. The only American attack near the town on 11 April was thirteen kilometres further to the west, and the target was the big house, Sheikh Malik's fam-ily home. The result was an atrocity that in the roiling Iraq crisis went virtually unreported.

Twenty-two civilians died. They were mostly women and children and almost all were Malik's immediate relatives. They died as first one and then another five powerful explosions tore his home apart. Starting at the kitchen and store-rooms at one end, the house ruptured like a giant Chinese fire-cracker as the missiles forced their way through to the recep-tion rooms at the opposite end.

It had been one of the most imposing houses in the region. When I was there, the sight of the sandwiched concrete slabs, once the floors, compelled me into the rubble. The shredded remains of a woman's gold embroidered blouse lay tangled in broken cinder-blocks; shattered ceramic tiles were littered among the foam-stuffing ripped from a couch; there was a smiling Barbie doll in a yellow polka-dot dress, the heat of the blast fusing her blonde hair with the mangled plastic of an electrical fitting; here were the children's charred school books – spelling, natural history and mathematics; a couple of sexy, strappy women's shoes – disfigured; and, nearby, two tiny children's shoes – not even a pair between them.

I went to Ramadi towards the end of the Iraqi summer of 2003, seeking but not quite believing the story of Malik's death, which had been told to me in Amman by a former adviser to the Jordanian royal family. But the recollections of a young man named Fahal Abdul Hamid, a nephew of the dead sheikh, quickly made the events of terrible night all too real: "It was 2 a.m. and the house was crowded – more than fifty people. We tend to gather under one roof when we are afraid, but most of the men were in another building watching the war on satellite TV. There was a blast of light and a fog of dust; it was hard to breathe. I went towards the big house but not much of it was left. More than half of the victims were kids under the age of nine; Malik's six-month-old daughter was never found; his mother, his wife, his sister and four of his nieces died; I found my younger brother – dead. We thought we'd be safe because we had survived the first Gulf War and we believed the Americans had to know where Malik was. We have houses in Jordan, Syria and Egypt. We could have gone anywhere, but we chose to stay because the sheikh should be among his people when times are hard."

Months after the US strike on the big house, chaos still gripped the clan, which is a part of the powerful Dulame tribe that dominates al-Anbar province in the west of Iraq. The new sheikh, Malik's 33-year-old brother Hamad, had not yet come to terms with the death in the bombing of four of his daughters, all under the age of five, and the loss of his only son, aged two years. For the time being, it had fallen to Sheikh Abdul Hamid, the father of Fahal, to hold things together by stepping in to act as leader of the Kharbit clan.

The symbolic heart of an Iraqi tribe is its mudhef. It is here that the sheikh holds his daily court, dispensing largesse and receiving troubled tribesmen, passers-by and visiting dignitaries. To enter what was once Sheikh Malik's mudhef is to step into another world, a parallel universe to the one in which the Bush administration struggles to manipulate a Rubik's Cube of Sunni, Shiite and Kurdish elements, hoping to resolve them into a democratic whole. As the US focuses on its self-appointed task, around it, unseen, are the pillars of an ancient tribal society that, along with religious crossbeams of equal strength and proportions, are likely to doom the American quest.

When I visited Malik's mudhef, a feast was produced even though I had arrived unannounced and it was the middle of the day. The repast came on a platter so large that four retainers were required to carry it. The much-prized, locally grown Anbar rice was piled high on leathery Iraqi bread that had been soaked in a rich broth. Scattered on top of the rice were chunks of succulent mutton, surrounded by vegetable stew; a drizzle of melted sheep's-milk butter contributed an unmistakeable local flavour. The servants produced a fork and spoon, but the gathering was thrilled when I ate as they did, with my hands. A ceiling fan turned lazily and ineffectually in the fifty-degree heat. A layer of fine dust dulled the shine on the terrazzo floor and the walls and ceiling were smoke-stained from a corner hearth where the fire burns around the clock – all visitors, at any time, must be offered tea or coffee. Fahal, the nephew of the dead sheikh, pointed to the steel doors, making what turned out to be a tribal declaration of survival: "This mudhef is always open."

Malik, by all accounts, was a man of rare qualities. By tradition, the eldest son of a sheikh assumes the leadership on the death of his father, but Malik was handpicked as a child by his father ahead of his older brothers and groomed for leadership. Thirty-five years old when he died, he was a shrewd tribal chief and businessman. His first love, though, was desert hunting. As he talked about this aspect of his uncle's world, Fahal's voice quavered: "He loved to hunt with his eagles. But a few days after the American attack, we had to set the birds free. They reminded us too much of Malik and, when he let them go, my father said: 'Your owner is free and now you must join him.'" Family members offered a litany of reasons for the sheikh's decision to become a US agent: the regime was frustrating his business plans; he was tired of the suffering of ordinary Iraqis after more than a decade of UN sanctions; most of all he was tired of Saddam.

It is still not clear how, let alone why, the Americans came to destroy one of their key sources of information about Saddam and his regime. My inquiries bounced about the ether – emails to CENTCOM bunkers in Florida, Iraq, Kuwait and Qatar – before the final brush-off came from Major Michael C. Escudie of the US Air Force. Claiming that he did not have the resources to look into the death of Malik, he emailed, "It was a busy time with many sorties ... I do not have information that such an attack rose to the threshold of warranting an investigation." Signing off as "Major Scud", he referred me to a flood of military news releases from the time, all of which were archived on the internet: "If you look at them, you'd see that pin-pointing one of the 30-plus cordon-and-knock missions on homes would be a challenge."

It seemed incredible to me that someone who had already been so useful to the Americans, and who could have been even more useful in advising them how best to gain some degree of acceptance in the most hostile territory in Iraq, could be killed without so much as an apology. Was it simply a colossal blunder? Perhaps. Yet Malik's death was not without consequence, and the episode opens a window onto the American attempt to impose its version of democracy in a lonely place where it needs all the friends it can get.

Sheikh Abdul Hamid, the man who temporarily took over leadership of the tribe in the months after the attack, had his own theory about the bombing. Astonishingly, given the personal catastrophe involved, he did not blame the Americans. His reasoning lost none of its force as his son Fahal, a 29-year-old business studies graduate, translated into perfect English a classic tale of power and envy in the desert: "There are people here who want us out of the equation because we are a strong family," he said. "Knowing that the Americans would bomb, they told them that Saddam was on our property. We know who they are, and we don't believe that the Americans are our enemies." The sheikh became too distressed to continue, and Fahal concluded his father's story in a way that knotted together many of the complex forces at work in tribal Iraq: "At first we felt this huge, devastating rage. But Dad is working to divert the anger – this family has not been targeted by the US, but by some of the local sheikhs who don't want us here. They are not of our clan; but they are of our tribe. So we must prove that even though Malik and the others are dead, this mudhef is always open. The family is alive – we are still here and we are strong."

TRIBES OF IRAQ

In the new Iraq, the US is caught in a pincers of its own making, between the tribes and the mosque. The Americans thought that both of these powers could be ignored as they dreamily set about crafting a secular administration that would be dominated by the hand-picked exiles Washington had air-lifted into the country as the dust of war settled in the spring of 2003. They feared that if liberated Iraqis were left to their own devices, the mullahs would demand an Iranian-style theocracy and the tribesmen would emulate the Afghan warlords with whom the US was still wrestling further to the east, in Afghanistan. These assumptions denied many tribal leaders a seat at the table in the early days of what the US calls "Iraqi freedom".

The Pentagon drove the whole exercise. It did not publish its blueprint for Iraq, but investigative reports by The Atlantic Monthly and The New Yorker leave little doubt that the neoconservative ideology of Dick Cheney, Donald Rumsfeld and Paul Wolfowitz took no account of the people and culture of Iraq. They junked years of informed State Department planning for the new state and instead approached their newly acquired patch of the Middle East as a greenfields site on which they believed they could build their democracy mall without planning approval. Seized more by the notion of democracy as a poison for Saddam Hussein than as a nourishment for his people, they marched on Baghdad with no plan other than to get rid of him.

In hindsight, the decision to exclude key Iraqi players has come at a huge cost. Iraqis use the same word for the men who wield tribal and religious power – sheikh – and it is these leaders who are manipulating war and politics as the Americans dig themselves deeper into the mire. Much of the most violent resistance to the US occupation comes from the minority Sunni tribes of central Iraq, while, with one critical exception, the religious leadership of the majority Shiite population, in the south, has resisted the temptation to resort to violence and instead fights with remarkable political skill to thwart US designs for the shape of their new government. The date – 30 June 2004 – rapidly approaches when the US will return to Iraqis a highly qualified sovereign power over their country.

The tribes are the foundation layer in Iraqi society – bedrock under the bedrock. Had there not been a decision by the sheikhs that Saddam Hussein was finished, the US might have met an Iraqi military machine that was prepared to stand and fight in March 2003 – with far bloodier consequences than Washington's "good war" in fact produced. More importantly, if the Americans had not been so reluctant to parlay with the sheikhs, they would have found them to be extraordinarily powerful allies in the aftermath of the war, as opposed to the sullen bystanders that many have become in the face of perceived US insolence and indifference.

In the wake of the overthrow of Saddam Hussein, the Western examination of Iraq is intense. Much of it, however, is also narrow and partisan. Even the most constructive criticism of the US occupation is turned on its head and ridiculed as support for the toppled dictator or endorsement of the activities of international terrorists in Iraq and elsewhere. Most in the West have been slow to recognise the inordinate power of the tribal sheikhs – men like Malik and Sheikh Abdul Hamid – or to realise how their power could have been harnessed to make a success of a military occupation that now seems like a very bad idea.

In Iraq and the Middle East, there are academics and experts in the service of governments – Arabic and American – who argue that the men in white robes and doily-like hats have the power to scale back, if not to end, the bloody resistance that cripples the rebuilding of Iraq. Several well-placed analysts argue that the sheikhs' tolerance of the deadly attacks on the US, and their sheltering of the fugitive Saddam Hussein until his capture in December 2003, have amounted to a calculated bid to win US recognition of their traditional leadership role in Iraqi society; and, more pertinently, their role as keepers of the peace. These experts argue that it is the sheikhs, not the US forces, who will create a secure environment in which the reconstruction of Iraq might develop the momentum that is essential to sustaining it. It follows that if they are ignored, they have the power to wreck any US designs for Iraq.

The sheikhs deny all of this, with a wave of their white-cuffed hands. Nevertheless, a striking continuity in more than half a dozen interviews with tribal sheikhs across the Sunni Triangle and the Shiite south – both self-proclaimed friends and foes of Washington – was the consistent refusal to condemn violence against the US forces in Iraq. In Malik's mudhef at Ramadi, Sheikh Abdul Hamid seemed to want to duck the issue altogether, when he told me, "I can't tell you what will happen with the resistance – you ask the Iraqi people." But then he complicated what might have been a straight answer to a simple question: "This is a trick question, because it suggests that we are behind the resistance." His protests sounded even more hollow when others in the mudhef revealed that on the previous day he had presided over a meeting of sheikhs from the region to deal with a pitch from a Turkish business delegation that wanted to bid for reconstruction contracts in the area. In the face of rising violence against foreign contractors, the Turks wanted the sheikhs' protection for their men and equipment. I was informed by someone who had attended the meeting, "They decided that if they allowed the Turks to come here, they would be seen to be working with the US and to be in favour of the occupation. So the sheikhs said no."

I found the same indifference at Abu Ghraib, just beyond the western fringe of Baghdad's urban sprawl. The town's US-appointed mayor, Sheikh Dhari Khamis al-Dhari, was ambivalent about the insurgency, and certainly would not go out of his way to condemn it. He explained in some detail how a mix of desperation brought on by Iraq's post-war economic crisis and deep-seated resentment of any foreign occupation had understandably fuelled the resistance. A few days later, in a village near Tikrit, Sheikh Ali Hussein al-Nida, one of the sheikhs of Saddam Hussein's own al-Bu Nasir tribe, harked back to the 1920s tribal resistance to the

British occupation of Iraq before warning that attacks on the US would not peter out. Sheikh Ali seemed to be arguing the case for all the sheikhs when he told me, "If the US does not quickly impose law and order, the tribes will do something very great against them. We all have weapons – they are a part of our lives; as he has bread, so an Iraqi has a weapon."

The unfolding of events in Iraq led me to the tribes before the mosques, because it was in the so-called Sunni Triangle, sprawling north and west from Baghdad, that the US faced the strongest resistance in the months after Saddam was toppled. At the time, the Shiites in the south were sitting on their hands, seeing what the Americans might make of their first months in Iraq, and what Washington would make of them, the new holders of the democratic majority.

Grasping the weight of the sheikhs' power, and understanding how they use it to direct the lives of their tribesmen or congregations, requires a sense of their anthropological history. Use your mind's eye to erase the existing national boundaries in the region. These are mere lines in the sand, drawn in the 1920s during earlier Western efforts to protect vested interests, principally oil. For centuries before that, what we now call the Middle East was carved into warring tribal fiefdoms.

The tribal sheikhs were born to rule according to ancient desert customs that are as alien to Washington and Westminster as Bondi is to Baghdad. Throughout the history of their region, the sheikhs have been the powerbrokers, deciding who would reign between the great rivers, the Tigris and the Euphrates. For centuries, they have been the swing voters in a land that has stubbornly resisted all attempts to import democracy. Their power and territorial grip may seem to be diminished today, but they still have a grip on the life of their people that goes to questions of life and death.

There are approximately 150 tribes in today's Iraq, and the sheikhs of perhaps thirty to forty of these tribes form a heavyweight division that presides over the affairs of 2000 clans and sub-tribes. In all, they speak for as much as three-quarters of the country's 25 million people. While the majority of the population might live in the cities, the nature of the tribes is best explored in rural Iraq. The code by which they live is enduring. It is romantic and it is brutal; pride and honour rule the sheikhs' hearts; survival and revenge rule their heads. A common Iraqi refrain is: "They are from the country – real men!"

In the *mudhef* of the late Sheikh Malik, I asked Abdul Hamid about the qualities that made a good sheikh. He singled out self-respect, and he made his point by recounting the story of an astonishing confrontation, in the early days of the US-led invasion of Iraq in 2003, between Saddam Hussein's tyrannical cousin, Ali Hassan al-Majid, better known as Chemical Ali, and a sheikh of the Bazoon tribe in southern Iraq. The story is rich in both the violence and deep sense of tribal priorities that shape Iraqi life. He began: "Al-Majid, whom Saddam charged with defending the south, demanded that as the Iraqis lined up to face the Americans, the Bazooni tribesmen should march in front. But the sheikh said, 'No – we should walk side by side.' Al-Majid was angry and he started shooting, killing the sheikh's son. The sheikh's response was to tell al-Majid, 'We're fighting a foreign force now; we'll have to settle this dispute after the war.' He could have shot al-Majid on the spot, but not in the face of the bigger task of war against the US." The storyteller sipped his tea, allowing me to digest the meaning of his tale before concluding with much pride, "We are descendants of the warriors of Bedouin times. You have to be a member of a tribe, otherwise who will stand up for you in a time of need?"

The tribes pre-date Islam. The forefathers of those who live in today's Iraq migrated from the arid Arabian Peninsula – what is now Saudi Arabia. They were seeking the bountiful waters of the Tigris and the Euphrates, and over time they became one of the great constants in the life of a region wracked by conflict, a global patch in which, according to an American Arabist who requested anonymity because he is employed by the US occupation authority in Baghdad, governments have made it their business to use and control the centrifugal impulses of tribal society as best they can. "Saddam did this pretty well," he told me in an interview in the main US compound in Baghdad. Today's American occupiers are not the first to challenge the tribes. Mohammed, the prophet, railed against what he called their "rotten ways". The British thought they could be co-opted against the Ottoman Empire. They could, but only briefly, while they faced a common enemy in Istanbul, and in 1920 the tribes revolted against London too. So began a cruel 38-year war of attrition to rid old Mesopotamia of the British and their influence.

Today's sheikhs lounge on the cushions and richly coloured carpets of their mudhefs and speak about legendary figures in their history as though they knew them personally: St John Philby – the father of the spy of the same name, who careered about the deserts on a motorbike, a British diplomat in leathers who drew lines in the sand that became today's oft-disputed national borders; Gertrude Bell – Arabist, diplomat and herself a spy who was dubbed the uncrowned queen of Iraq; and the man in whose shadow they all walked, Lawrence of Arabia.

T.E. Lawrence's 1920 dismissal of Britain's lunge at Iraq as "not far from a disaster" proved to be correct. Now, more than eighty years later and a year after Washington's lunge at Saddam Hussein, there's a curious indifference in the US bunkers in Baghdad to the stark lessons of Iraqi history. But if they cared to look back, the Americans might be struck by the resonance of Lawrence's warning that the people of Britain had been led into a Mesopotamian trap: "They have been tricked into it by a steady withholding of information. Things are far worse than we have been told." Had they cared to probe the past, Washington's strategists might have paused over the caustic explanation for the British disaster given by the reed-like Gertrude Bell, in a letter she wrote from Baghdad in the 1920s: "I suppose we have underestimated the fact that this country is really an inchoate mass of tribes which can't as yet be reduced to any system. The Turks didn't govern, and we have tried to govern – and failed."

Saddam Hussein failed too. Those of us who sat through the 2003 war in Baghdad, waiting for the American forces to arrive in the capital, listened in puzzlement to the dictator's speeches, which invariably opened with a litany of flowery greetings to individual tribes. Later it was explained to me that what Saddam was doing was appealing for them to stand with him, but he had left his run too late. As ever, the tribes were as pragmatic as they were commercial – and as far as Saddam was concerned, their loyalty had become wafer-thin. They were in no mood to respond to his last, empty entreaties; as they saw it, there was little left to be squeezed from Saddam, so why would they order their brothers and sons to line up to fight for him? More importantly, why protect him after the war – unless, that is, he could serve as a bargaining chip in their dealings with the new American overlords?

As the Americans pushed north into Iraq from Kuwait, they did encounter some resistance, but the sheikhs now argue that this had more to do with maintaining self-respect in the face of a foreign invasion than with any impulse to defend their president. At the time of our interview Saddam was still on the run, but Sheikh Abdul Hamid was anything but sentimental: "Our decision not to fight for Saddam was spontaneous. It's not that we didn't love him or that we did love George Bush. We simply chose the stronger side and we did it for self-preservation." The sheikhs could see that Saddam Hussein would go down, but the tribes of Iraq would not go down with him; not when they were already dreaming about the deals they might strike with the forces of the richest and most powerful empire of all time, then marching on Baghdad. The refusal by the US to engage in the barter process anticipated by the sheikhs explains much of their disgust with Iraq's liberators. As we dug our hands into the rice at Sheikh Abdul Hamid's table, he voiced a classic sheikh's caution for Iraq's new American occupiers: "Remember, you can have an alliance with us, but you can't depend on us forever."

Saddam could see in the sheikhs what Washington could not see at first, and only recently has shown some signs of understanding. In the words of one of Saddam's biographers, Said K. Aburish, "Iraqi family and tribal connections are supreme. They come ahead of ideology. They come ahead of commitment to the nation-state; they come ahead of all commitments." Sheikh Abdul Hamid holds the same view, but he expresses it from the sheikh's perspective: "Saddam had more power over this land than the US does at present and even he had to keep the sheikhs on side. Instead of us, the US has chosen to deal with a bunch of thieves" – by which he meant the returned exiles and some stooge sheikhs appointed by Saddam – "who command no respect. They refuse to ask us for help."

Coming from the tribes himself, Saddam was acutely aware of the potency of tribal power, so much so that he set out to destroy what was left of the tribes in the early years of his regime. He executed and jailed key figures. He outlawed significant elements of tribal culture and ordered large internal migrations in the hope of diluting the power of individual sheikhs. It was a mark of his desperation that he finally turned to them when confronted by the near collapse of the state around him, as his economy crumbled and internal security fragmented after his disastrous 1980s war against Iran and the Kuwait debacle in 1991. The result was a power-sharing deal that stirred tribal memories of a more glorious and powerful past. Saddam's crippled forces were unable to secure the country, and so he paid the sheikhs to organise their tribesmen to do what they saw as their traditional law-and-order duty. A prominent sheikh told me that, "Saddam lavished gifts on the trusted sheikhs – three and four cars and a house for a general or for high-ranking party members who were in the tribes. He'd give them farms and write off their bad debts. They'd get Nissan or Toyota pickups, sometimes even a Land Cruiser. After a meeting, he'd send them a gift of maybe five million dinars; suddenly, schools and hospitals were being built in their towns and villages and farm debts were being written off."

For the sheikhs it was a dangerous balancing act. Sheikh Abdul Hamid explained how Saddam, his sons and their cronies would commandeer millions of dollars as their cut of a business deal or how they would punish a sheikh simply by refusing to authorise the payment of a state debt to the sheikh's business. His face framed by the tails of his red-and-white checked *keffiyeh* and his gimlet eyes glinting beneath a monk's grey fringe, Sheikh Abdul Hamid confided, "Till the fall of Baghdad all the sheikhs were allied to Saddam by money or fear. We were locked into a life of gifts and threats." They understood only too well that survival for Saddam invariably meant revenge against them later on. This wily old sheikh had been thrown into prison by Saddam and only the power of his tribe had forced his release; and in the run-up to the war, the regime had frozen the multi-million dollar assets of his family's construction, farming and oil services business. The sheikhs knew all along that the stronger they became in a new environment in which Hussein nurtured the tribes, the more he would come to suspect them. Another old Iraqi put it this way for me: "Saddam Hussein practiced the Arab policy of the sword and the dinar – if you are with him you will be rich; if you are against him he will cut your throat."

Dhlo'iya, about 120 kilometres north of Baghdad, is one of the villages in which Saddam is said to have sought refuge after an attempt on his life in the early 1980s. The geography would have been a great comfort to the former president; nestled deep in a luxuriant, tight U-shaped bend in the Tigris River, it is a small village that can be approached from only one side, giving it ample protection. People in neighbouring areas now speak gleefully about the abrupt end to Saddam's largesse for the locals. In July 2003, Sheikh Sedam Kahiya, from the al-Bu Amir tribe, told a researcher for the International Crisis Group, "Saddam loved these tribal domains for their date palms, water and the tribal way of life. He assisted Dhlo'iya beyond imagination – its residents are extremely unhappy now." What drew me to the village was a tragedy of biblical proportions – the death in July 2003 of 27-year-old Sabah Kerbul and what it revealed about the remarkable power of a Sunni sheikh of the al-Jabouri people, the biggest tribe in Iraq.

Sheikh Hamid Shwash al-Jabouri, a university-educated man, decreed that the father of Sabah Kerbul must execute his son after he had been accused of collaborating with US forces in the days before and after a massive American raid on the village in the previous month. Hussein Tallef Abdullah, a cousin of the accused man and a lawyer, told me that, "The whole village was talking about what Sabah had done. The tribes were boiling for revenge – people were dead, our women had been shamed and the furniture in their homes had been broken by the US raiding parties. Sabah Kerbul's father was threatened with death. Then they talked about evicting the family from the village and destroying their house. Unless his father agreed to kill Sabah, some wanted the whole family to die." At this point, Abdullah reduced the family's crisis to a gritty tribal equation: "Sabah was accused by very powerful sheikhs and very powerful members of the community. We are a small family, we have few uncles and no fighters, so we had to accept what was to happen."

A couple of weeks after my first visit to Dhlo'iya I returned, hoping to meet the sheikh who had the power to order Sabah Kerbul's execution. Sheikh Shwash was at home, sitting cross-legged on a vine-fringed verandah at the rear of his farm property, where date palms stood tall over dusty orange groves. His white headdress fell to the shoulders of his grey dishdasha as he discussed the post-war crisis with a gathering of about fifteen men, all dressed in the varying putty and buff shades of the local landscape. They nodded deferentially when the 54-year-old sheikh declared, "It's a mess. We don't have power, water or fuel. So our crops and orchards are dying and there are no jobs for the people." Sheikh Shwash said those around him were a mix of relatives and members of the al-Jabouri tribe. No one else dared to talk during my five-hour visit, but despite all the evidence to the contrary, the sheikh defended the gathering as an open forum: "This meeting is a daily custom. We discuss everything. It's like a school, but everyone gets to talk, so it is fully democratic as well."

Like the other sheikhs, Shwash emphasised that leadership and justice were the fulcrums of tribal life. He had just returned from nearby Khazrag, where he had mediated in a dispute that threatened to engulf members of his own al-Jabouri tribe and their al-Bidjuwari neighbours in war. "It was a murder. Someone killed a person so we had to get them to agree to pay three million Iraqi dinars to the family of the victim." As a soot-blackened coffee pot which had done the rounds of this *mudhef* for more than 100 years went around again, the sheikh explained some of the basics of tribal justice. A dispute over a personal attack might be settled by the payment of a sum of money; higher if the attack happened by night. The theft of a box of oranges might be settled by the payment to the victim of a sheep.

When I raised the topic of the execution of Sabah Kerbul, he became crotchety: "I knew you were coming to this question!" Then the man who all in the village believe ordered the young man's death blithely mounted a circuitous argument denouncing Kerbul's character and claiming that the village was better off without him. Any court would have found him guilty, the sheikh insisted. He offered an improbable account of what had happened: "Sabah was a bad guy and people were very upset. His father came to me and said he was so ashamed that he would chop off Sabah's head and parade it around the tribe. There was no meeting. And I didn't have to make a decision, because I had the word of his father that he would kill him. Anything else you hear is the imaginings of a distraught father, but the relationship between us is bigger than any trouble. His father and I will be able to jump over this."

Clearly uncomfortable with the discussion, he changed the subject by producing an elaborate chart of his family tree going back 800 years. It allowed him to speak of things no member of the tribe would have dared to discuss with a foreign reporter before the overthrow of Saddam Hussein and, indirectly, to challenge the claims by neighbouring tribes that his people had done well under Saddam. As a gentle breeze nudged the date palms that stood like guards around the property, he told the recent history of the tribe. "Our people became second-class citizens because we dared to say no to Saddam. We were part of a movement inside the army in 1989 that tried to kill him by copying the 1981 assassination of Anwar Sadat." He identified Suttam al-Jabouri as a member of the tribe who was among those plotting against Saddam. When I enquired as to his fate, he made a silent but powerful slashing motion across his own throat before advancing a decade to explain the outcome of another Jabouri-led coup attempt which Saddam had thwarted: "He dismissed every al-Jabouri member from any position of importance in the military, the government and the Baath Party. In Tikrit, where he was always building palaces and military complexes, the contractors were forbidden to employ Egyptians, Kurds and members of the al-Jabouri tribe."

Asked about the future of the tribes in a US-imposed, Western-style democracy, the sheikh gave a cryptic response. "The tribes will work for the Iraqi people," he said too smoothly. Here is a critical issue for the new Iraq. Where is the natural fit between a culture of hereditary, born-to-rule sheikhs, blood money and revenge killings on the one hand, and Western democratic fundamentals such as due process and one-man, one-vote on the other? If they go along with the proposed US democracy, will the sheikhs simply hijack the process to perpetuate their own form of autocracy? Or will the American dream become an imposed reality, drawing younger Iraqis away to Western values and sensibilities? At Ramadi, this was a point Sheikh Abdul Hamid al-Kharbit had confronted head-on, warning sharply, "If they force democracy on us there will be chaos. It won't work because we have a lot of tribes and pre-existing relations that are very complex." He became melodramatic, as he ticked off Washington: "The Iraqi people are like lions in a cage – let them out and they will even eat their trainer. We're wild people, we tend to violence and our history shows that Iraq can work only as a kingdom or a dictatorship." On the banks of the Tigris, Sheikh Shwash, the executioner, deferred to the silent majority around him when I asked if he would be able to command the votes of all of the al-Jabouri tribe if he decided to run for elected office. Modesty required him to mutter, "I don't know." When I asked if I could put the question to the rest of the gathering, he nodded before one of them insisted, "He will be elected by the al-Jabouri people. We will elect him because he has good judgement and a lively brain."

Sounding every bit the canny diplomat, Sheikh Shwash went on to describe the man running the US occupation of Iraq, Paul Bremer, as "a gentleman ... not a bureaucrat". I was surprised – surely for a respected Iraqi sheikh this was a generous view of the head of a hated occupation force? He explained with a broad smile, "In the first period with anyone, we always act and behave as friends because of our morals, religion and manners. So, when we first meet, we will start with the greeting *Salam Allaykum* – 'Peace be upon you.' If they don't live up to our expectations, that is the time when we will decide what to do. After every event there is a discussion ... the US can make enemies here just as easily as they can make friends. But after four months of this occupation, my hopes for friendship are failing."

These are dangerous days for sheikhs who co-operate with the Americans. The two new mounds in the cemetery at Haditha, four hours drive north-west from Baghdad, are the graves of the late mayor Mohammed Nayil al-Jurayfi and his young son. Al-Jurayfi apparently made himself mayor in the days after the fall of Baghdad. Later, US commanders in the area and the sheikhs of his Jukaifa tribe endorsed his self-appointment, but clearly the gunmen disagreed. The lethal lesson is well taken – at Abu Ghraib, about thirty-five miles west of Baghdad, Dhari Khamis al-Dhari, who heads another US-appointed local council, has a holstered pistol slung on the back of his chair and a US tank outside his office. "This is a tribal area and people know me and they know that this council is trying to do good things," he says. "But some claim that we are collaborators and we all have received threats and warnings not to co-operate with the US or we will be eliminated." He pointed across the room at the council's manager of power and other services: "Look at Mr Jalil – you can see the bullet holes in his car!"

Al-Dhari is a sheikh of the Zoba'a tribe, and he invited me to sit in on a meeting of his council, where local affairs were conducted in a rat-a-tat fashion. There was no agenda, people walked in, had a say, made a plea and left – empty-handed, more often than not. The minutiae of the business was revealing. A ceiling fan and a clunking evaporative air-conditioner, which was propped up outside an open window, struggled to cool the bunker-like municipal HQ, but when the power failed for the third time in an hour, both gave up the ghost. Two US Army officers marched in. They outlined a proposal for a new water treatment plant, including its location, capacity and the reaction, so far, of the locals. Al-Dhari gave them a long look. He had only one condition: "We will proceed, as long as it doesn't cost us a cent!" Most remarkable in this exchange was the revelation that at least some of the American invaders had worked out how to get things done quickly – fall in behind the authority of the local sheikh.

Sixty-four-year-old al-Dhari sat behind his desk, an ear on the discussions among his councillors – four of the eight are his cousins – as he signed and stamped hand-written orders and documents put before him. When I had first met him in Baghdad three weeks earlier he was in Western dress, but he had warned me that things would be different in Abu Ghraib. Here he was wearing the full traditional dress – a flowing white *dishdasha* and a white-on-white chequered *keffiyeh* on which, during a pause in the business of the council, a fly waltzed along one of its hand-stitched edges. The ubiquitous Thuraya satellite phone sat on the left of the desk; the stamp of his office was on the right. A row between two farmers over the position of a new well was put to one side so that the council could deal with the complaint of a bruised and bandaged young man who was demanding that al-Dhari sign a letter accusing American soldiers of beating him up. The man told his story in dramatic gestures, lifting various parts of his clothing to reveal more scratches, grazes and bruises. He pointed an imaginary rifle; he went through the motions of being made to remove his trousers and forced to lie on the ground, and of being denied a drink of water. Sheikh Dhari doubted that he was hearing the full story, but he signed the letter and sent the man off to see the Americans, knowing full well that they would bat it back to him at their next regular meeting. Rat-a-tat-tat, they stream through that door. The council's irrigation manager tried to complain that his Nissan pickup had been stolen at gunpoint the previous evening, but he got little sympathy from al-Dhari – only days earlier his own BMW sedan had been stolen while a machine-gun was held to his head in broad daylight in the streets of Baghdad.

Finally there was a lull and al-Dhari spoke about his relationship with the local American commanders. "It was reported that I welcomed the US – this is not true; I'm not a candidate for the Americans. And I told them when they came here that if they could not work with the tribes, their enterprise would fail. They don't understand the North American Indian tribes any more than they understand the Iraqi tribes," he said dismissively, going on to illustrate his own knowledge by naming a dozen Native American tribes. He got up a head of steam: "When I first met the Americans in mid-April, I asked them to keep in mind that they come from a different country and tradition and could they, please, try to understand our people and our way of life, our tradition, our religion and our rites. I told them, 'If you respect the Iraqi people, they will leave you alone.'" He pulled at his own headdress: "Even this – it's not just to cover my head. It's a headdress that is a part of our pride and dignity and people have been killed for throwing another man's to the floor." He seemed to want me to ask the obvious, so I did: were the Americans showing him the respect he requested? He paused for a long time: "Dignity and respect is what I asked for and I regret that in too many cases the answer is no; we are not treated with dignity and respect. We treat the elderly with great respect in this area. None of them are left in the streets and children do not make fun of them. But now, Iraqi boys and girls are made to see their fathers being dragged from cars and made to lie on their bellies on the street and I've been told often enough that the soldiers then put their boots on the Iraqi's head or the back of their neck. In the US, do they handcuff and blindfold women and make them sit in the sun for hours, even when they are pregnant? Some of the Americans are polite, friendly even. But many of them do things with little thought for the reputation of the US. They have dropped out of college or school and they have no choice but to join the army."

Al-Dhari sees his council through tribal eyes: "We're like a small government – we try to run everything ... 140 schools, police, postal services and colleges. We have maybe one million people. We have lots of factories and hundreds of villages." But the mayor seemed to have forgotten something. Abu Ghraib is known around the world as one of the darkest corners of what was Saddam Hussein's realm, because it was here that he imprisoned and executed his opponents by the tens of thousands. "Oh, the prison," he said, seeming not to recollect that even some of his own friends and many of his tribesmen had died in its cells. "It was the biggest in Iraq. Some people are sorry it's closed because prison visitors from all over the country used to spend money in local shops and hotels." This was just before the US decided – with incredible insensitivity – that it would use Saddam's prison as its own, and months before the US would be engulfed in its own abuse scandal at Abu Ghraib. I attempted to elicit a more thoughtful response by asking about his personal reaction to having such a dark stain from Saddam's era on the town. The mayor would not be provoked: "They took our land for the jail, even for the jailer's houses and they didn't pay us. But the prison itself doesn't cause embarrassment locally – people just don't talk about it."

In Abu Ghraib, the Americans were helping to build a new street market to stop vendors from encroaching on the highway running through the town. They were repairing the sewerage system and servicing trucks and pumps for al-Dhari's municipal council. What did the tribes' acceptance of such US efforts amount to? I told the mayor about a conversation I had had in Amman, on the way to Baghdad in the summer of 2003, with a Jordanian colleague who insisted that the tribes could make or break

Washington in Iraq. She had argued that a sheikh was essentially driven by greed and his own need to survive. In consequence, he would accept whatever largesse he could from whomever he could; and by distributing it around the tribe he would be well thought of and command the gratitude and loyalty of his people. Sheikh Dhari, who was educated by the Jesuits in Baghdad and later completed his university studies in Germany, was not offended. In fact, he agreed and expanded on the argument in his perfect English: "Because we accept these benefits from the US, it does not mean that we accept the Americans. We might have a fancy Western name, but this council is tribal. You have to have the backing of the tribes to get anything done in this area. People don't respect me because I'm the head of the council; it's because I'm a sheikh of the Zoba'a tribe."

There is more to this sheikh's personal story. For many Iraqis, Sheikh Dhari's grandfather is a revered national hero and patriot. In August 1920, the old man sparked a tribal revolt against the British when he used a Persian-made Brno rifle to assassinate a British officer, the fabled Colonel Gerard Leachman. A contemporary of T.E. Lawrence, Leachman took to wearing Arab dress as he trekked the uncharted deserts of Mesopotamia by camel and horse, reporting back to London on how the Arab tribes might be used to advance British interests in the dying days of the Ottoman Empire. When Britain finally took control of what was to become Iraq, Leachman stayed on, acquiring a reputation for ruthlessness and brutality as he put down Arab uprisings. At this point, the sheikh's history lesson was interrupted by the arrival in his office of a toss-haired Westerner – Andy Morrison, a Baghdad-based official of Washington's occupation authority, the CPA. His arrival prompted Sheikh Dhari to go into even greater detail in describing his grandfather's exploits. He seemed overly keen to get his story across to this representative of a newly arrived occupation force. Slightly nonplussed, Morrison asked, "Why did your grandfather kill him?" Dhari accepted the invitation with glee: "Leachman was arrogant and insulting in his treatment of the sheikhs and my grandfather could not take it any more. A very good film was made about this. I'll see if I can arrange the loan of a video copy of it for you." Morrison, seemingly oblivious to the import of the message that Dhari had just delivered to him, asked, "You don't have it on DVD, do you?"

History resonates in a particular way for the Dhari clan. The mayor sat back and dwelt on this topic: "The British said they came as liberators, but they stayed for forty years. I hope this history is not repeated because Iraq will not tolerate a long-term American occupation. Lawrence of Arabia and Leachman knew how to use the tribes. I don't have a sense that the US knows us in the same way. Unlike Lawrence, the Americans who are here believe what their superiors tell them. And we can't expect them to get to know us, because they keep rotating the officers, all of whom are sent here to do as they are told."

Iraqis are acutely aware of their own history. Many of them are buoyed by its messages and warnings, as much for what they might say to Iraqis as to the US occupation forces. In the 1920s the British tricked the Shiite majority by rigging election rules to their disadvantage. When the Shiite clergy demanded that the rules be rewritten, the British declared key Shiite imams to be "citizens of Persia" and bundled them into exile. The British got the king they wanted: the non-Iraqi Prince Faisal I of the Hashemites was imported from what became Jordan; and they got the rigged parliament that they worked so hard to achieve. Yet they never won the hearts and minds of the Iraqi people. Just as the Americans have tried to rig the post-war Iraqi government with their air-lift of returned exiles, the British followed a plan that, in the words of one historian, "relied heavily on putting pliable but unpopular Arabs in sham authority". Scholars blame this approach for the 1920s revolt and the instability that followed. Even the new king despaired. Lamenting the weakness of his regime in 1933, he hid none of his bitterness at the poison chalice he had accepted from London: "(The Iraqis) are unimaginable masses of human beings devoid of any patriotic ideas ... prone to anarchy and perpetually ready to rise against any government whatsoever."

THE SHEIKHS' PLOT

In Khaldiya, west of Baghdad, it's a war of nerves. A crater three metres deep marks the explosion of a careering car-bomb that the local police knew was inevitable; and just across, and down a highway that cuts through this small town between Ramadi and Falluja, was the home of a man the US suspected could help bring an end to these relentless attacks, a tribal sheikh by the name of Fanar al-Kharbit. My inquiries about a picture on the wall of his *mudhef* accidentally revealed that Sheikh Fanar was a cousin of the victim of the American bombs west of Ramadi on 11 April, the much-loved Sheikh Malik.

There is little doubt that as a tribal leader in the Sunni hotbed between Ramadi and Falluja, Sheikh Fanar is a man who knows more than he lets on. And there's the rub — the US had him figured as a potential source of what it likes to call "actionable intelligence", but they didn't have enough to pull him in. American tanks rumbled into his walled compound on the banks of the Euphrates River no less than seven times in December 2003, soldiers tumbling out to rummage through his home while, he says, telling him all the time to "shut up". The sheikh is still full of hard talk, but those who know him said that at the time of the raids he was reduced to a shadow of his former self. Once one of the richest men in Iraq, he used to strut in crisp traditional dress and hobnob with the most senior elements of the regime; Saddam Hussein was a frequent guest at his table till a falling-out over business in the early '90s. When we first met a few months into the US occupation, however, he was ill-kempt and gaunt; more like a bewildered shepherd, seemingly lost as he sat on his haunches against the front wall of his home compound, glowering at each passing American convoy.

It is impossible to verify the seemingly fantastic stories told to me by this obviously embittered man. In several of our encounters, however, Sheikh Fanar detailed the activities of his family in going abroad to meet US agents and spiriting into Iraq CIA operatives in the guise of visiting

American businessmen. He also described a tribal plot to hijack eight Iraqi Air Force bombers for an attack on Saddam's palaces as a prelude to a coup only days before the start of the US-led invasion on 20 March 2003. At first the sheikh was guarded, but once he understood that I had pieced together much of his cousin's story from other sources, he suggested that I return to his *mudhef* a week later, when four of us would sit down to a table that groaned under the load of an exotic Arabic feast which was served in fifty-five dishes. I was in the bosom of the Iraqi tribes ... from the pattern of tiny tattooed dots on Sheikh Fanar's wrist and ankle, to a painting on the wall of a long, black Bedouin tent, camels and date palms and a family engrossed in camp life, all under a burning blue sky. For a moment I felt myself to be a long way from the tension and violence of today's Iraq.

Sheikh Fanar would not reveal the details of his cousin Malik's meetings with US agents in Jordan, but he said that the two of them were part of a group of sheikhs who had concluded that Saddam was finished, but they wanted Iraqis, not foreigners, to bring him down. The CIA had initiated the contact with Sheikh Malik, and in 1998 and again in 2000 the family's business vehicles were used several times to ferry men, who openly admitted that they worked for the CIA, from the Jordan–Iraq border to Baghdad for secret meetings with senior Iraqis, including Saddam's deputy, Tariq Aziz, and the head of the Iraqi secret service.

He described a series of frenetic meetings – in Falluja, Baghdad at the Habania air force base, near his home – as plans for the coup came together. He said, "We had the pilots prepared – they would bomb the palaces and the TV station. When the US invasion started, we were still negotiating with some of the army generals to mount ground attacks on the palaces and to maintain law and order in Baghdad in the aftermath of our bombings. We had a special mobile radio station that was to keep the people informed ... but it all needed a few more weeks to make it happen."

Sheikh Fanar said that Malik had been out of the country when the war started, but he had returned late in March for yet another last-ditch attempt to get Saddam to go quietly. They had been summoned to a meeting in Baghdad with one of Saddam's sons-in-law, Jamal Mustafa, who wanted to appeal to them as tribal leaders to support Saddam in the face of the American invasion. His recall was vivid: "We started at the Baghdad Hotel, but the bombing came so close that we had to move to the al-Weia Club. Instead of offering help, we told Mustafa that Saddam should quit for the sake of his family and for all Iraqis. He was furious when we asked for a meeting with Saddam to put our argument face to face."

Fanar and Malik were so confident in their belief that Saddam Hussein could be talked into surrendering that before their meeting with the President's son-in-law they made contact with the Americans through an Iraqi friend they knew to be accompanying the US units then advancing on Baghdad from the west. Explaining that they needed to buy time, Fanar said that, "We asked the Americans for three days to allow us to change the regime. We received a message that they would give us the time, but on the second of the three days the Americans entered Baghdad. Liars!"

But hadn't the Americans achieved their objective? Wasn't Saddam gone? Sheikh Fanar went to the nub of the issue for many Iraqis: "We are ashamed that it was the US, not Iraqis who toppled Saddam. We are Arabs and we have a custom that does not allow outsiders to kill our enemies. This occupation is a cause for great shame for all Iraqis. The Americans did what Iraqis should have done and they are still here to remind us of it."

It was time to go. Sheikh Fanar repeated his view that the Iraqi insurgents were merely protecting their country: "This is not liberation; it is occupation ... we have left a dark room and gone into another that is even darker. But the US will fail in Iraq." As a wizened retainer opened the gates so that we could drive out of the compound, we received two pieces of advice. First, the five-year-old son of one of the gatemen told us that we should drive close to any American soldiers on the way back to Baghdad – so that we could shoot them. Second, as we set out on a stretch of highway where the Americans are subjected to intense road-side bombings, Sheikh Fanar uttered blunt words of warning: "Drive in the middle of the road."

The capture of Saddam in December 2003 put a brief spring in the step of the US leadership in Baghdad, but it also focused the glare of public attention on the clandestine Task Force 121, a mix of operatives from the US Defense Intelligence Agency, the CIA and Special Forces who were involved in the arrest. According to informed reports in the US, the task-force forms part of a campaign of covert war in Iraq. Its strategy – described by Seymour Hersh in *The New Yorker* as "pre-emptive man hunt-ing" – has rekindled unfavourable memories of Washington's Operation Phoenix in Vietnam, when Special Forces teams worked with Vietnamese agents to detain or kill those suspected of working or sympathising with the Vietcong. Somewhere between 20,000 and 40,000 Vietnamese are esti-mated to have been eliminated over five years, a troubling proportion of them for spurious reasons.

There is a parallel to be found in Iraq in the hatred between the major-ity Shiites and Kurds, on one hand, and the minority Sunnis who for decades mistreated the rest in the name of Saddam Hussein. There is a frightening risk that Task Force 121 will be sooled on to many Sunnis, perhaps people like Sheikh Fanar al-Kharbit, in settlement of personal grievances as much as for protection of national security.

"In the first few months relations with the US were friendly, but now they are trying to provoke me," Fanar told me in another meeting. He pointed to the charred remains of reed beds by the oozing Euphrates as it runs past his property, which he said he had been ordered to burn so that his activities might be observed more closely from US watch posts on a nearby bridge. "They are stupid, because they are listening to their spies who say bad things about me. I'm not a part of the resistance; but those who are, are just protecting their country. This is not liberation, it is an occupation. People are very tired after Saddam's three wars. I'm worried if the Americans keep attacking me, that my tribe will react, but for now I have told my people not to cause trouble." As is always the case in Iraq, it was difficult in first meetings to gauge the truth of Fanar's insistence that he was not a part of the resistance. I had concluded that he was, and that the difficulty he faced was that in running Saddam to ground, the Americans had revealed that they might have begun to grasp the power of Iraqi tribalism and to understand how it dovetailed with the resistance. Tracking more than 9000 people in tribal families loyal to Saddam, US intelligence officers had worked on four family names, detaining more than 1200 of them. The critical information on the hole in the ground in which Saddam hid was extracted only hours before the fallen dictator's arrest. It came from one of his most trusted tribal associates, whose name was on a list of twenty compiled from the 1200 in detention, as intelligence officers tested a theory that families that propped up Saddam in power were most likely to be protecting him on the run.

Fanar refuses to name the sheikh he believes to have shopped him and his family to the Americans, but around the time of Saddam's capture he told associates that he has commenced his own campaign of low-level retaliation. He had sent the sheikh in question, who lives in Ramadi, a gift of a black *abaya*, the unflattering and voluminous head-to-toe garment worn by more conservative Iraqi women, along with several lipsticks. Whatever he was up to, when I last visited Fanar al-Kharbit at his home at Khaldiya in the autumn of 2003, he seemed prepared to keep punching. As was his wont when he farewelled us, he returned to his place against the wall in the pale afternoon sun, throwing off another warning to the US: "I've told the Americans to get out of my neighbourhood. They wouldn't be here if I was a leader of the mujahideen." He paused for effect: "… and if they keep going like this, a lot more US soldiers will die."

We had met several times. The last I heard of Sheikh Fanar was in April 2004, when Salaam, the translator who had accompanied me on my first visit to the sheikh's home, reported excitedly that he had seen Fanar on the Arab satellite news service, al-Jazeera. He had been speaking on behalf of the fighters at Falluja. This was proof indeed of a great loss to the American occupation forces. Here was a man whose tribe and family had actively worked with the US against Saddam, who had risked their lives for Washington's Iraq agenda; but who in our last meeting had told me that he was duty bound to seek revenge for the death of his cousin. At the time, he was keeping his own counsel, telling me only, "Yes. Everything will be done at the right time."

THE SHIITES

The gold-leaf domes of the most sacred Shiite shrines in the world lure a constant procession of prayer and death, through the day and even into the night. On my first visit to Karbala, just weeks before the American invasion in 2003, four men with a coffin hoisted on their shoulders walked down the main street, followed by about 200 mourners, most of whom wore the green-banded fez that identifies them as direct descendants of the seventh-century holy men whose tombs beckon all Shiites to this forlorn corner of Iraq. A battered taxi circled the shrine, a coffin strapped to its roof-rack. Another procession arrived on foot, dozens of men silently slipping out of their sandals before lining up for prayers as a lone voice in their midst chanted through a loud-hailer. Minutes later, their place in the white marbled forecourt was taken by the loneliest death of the day – only four mourners, just enough to carry a coffin that was draped in a length of richly embroidered green cloth.

The shrines at Karbala that glorify the brothers Imam Abass and Imam Hussein are identical mosques, only 100 metres apart. As a gentle sun fought to break through muddy skies, they were utterly beautiful. Beneath the golden domes and minarets, the walls were a mesmerising riot of high-glazed blues and yellows, on which were inscribed thousands of lines from the Koran. Inside, behind the heavy brocade curtains that hung in a huge, ornate doorway, the walls and vaulted ceilings were covered in a mosaic of mirrored glass that sparkled in the light cast by dozens of chandeliers. In the centre was the green-lit tomb. Like the great cedar doors in the walls that enclose the mosque, the filigree panels of the tomb were buffed to a high sheen by the constant rubbing and kissing of the faithful, who reverentially touch the gold and silver latticework and then touch their faces in an endless quest for blessings.

Karbala was one of the great unknowns as the Americans entered Iraq, because of a short-lived revolt and its brutal suppression by Saddam Hussein in the weeks after the 1991 Gulf War. As Iraq braced for a new war early in 2003, many observers feared that these people would be unable to resist the urge to rise against Saddam once more. Human rights groups, diplomats and reporters had pieced together shocking accounts of the violence perpetrated by both sides in 1991. The Shiite population had erupted after decades of oppression at the hand of Saddam's Sunni-dominated regime, hanging twenty to thirty local leaders of the ruling Baath Party in a prayer room in the basement of the Imam Abass Mosque. Saddam retaliated, unleashing the best of his surviving troops with orders to bring into line both Karbala and the neighbouring city of Najaf. Much of the centre of Karbala was flattened by Saddam: the shrines were badly damaged, thousands of Shiite clerics were arrested and hundreds are said to have been executed; there was much indiscriminate shooting and death as Saddam's military moved about the city, with townspeople tied to the regime's tanks as human shields.

Najaf, 190 kilometres south of Baghdad, is holy to the Shiites because of the burial there – in an equally beautiful mosque to those in Karbala – of Imam Ali, the father of the imams buried at Karbala and a cousin and brother-in-law of Mohammed the Prophet. In this historic centre of learning, students were scattered and the holy libraries destroyed in Saddam's post-Kuwait crack-down. Later, in what was seen as a deliberate act of desecration, a highway was built across Wadi Salam, which, because of the desire of Shiites around the world to be buried in their holy cities, is the biggest cemetery in all the Middle East. Visitors to Karbala in the early 1990s likened the damage to that following a massive earthquake; it was intended, the Shiites claimed, to extinguish once and for all a longstanding campaign for a representative voice in the running of the country.

In the aftermath of the 1991 uprising, the two shrine cities were subjected to the carrot-and-stick treatment. Saddam donated hundreds of kilograms of gold to refurbish the shrines he had destroyed, and he rebuilt the centre of Karbala, although many Shiites were deeply offended by the loss of the Persian aspect that had once characterised parts of the city. And for all this, the United Nations Commission for Human Rights reported that high-ranking clerics continued to die in strange circumstances, often in unexplained traffic accidents. A UN report said at the time, "These murders are part of a systematic attack on the independent leadership of Shiite Muslims in Iraq."

Before the 2003 war, at least one of Saddam's city officials was having none of this talk of division. At the Karbala governate office, Kazum al-Aradi told me, "The people of this city have promised Saddam that Karbala will become a cemetery for any American or Australian soldiers who get this far into Iraq. Ask anyone in the streets and they will tell you this."

Indeed they did. Fifty senior clerics signed a petition of support for Saddam in their own blood, and in the streets people said that all of Iraq would fight for their president. Away from the hearing of the guide from Saddam's Information Ministry, however, several Shiites confided to me that they still had vivid memories of Washington's failure to back them in 1991. Depending on who spoke, these memories made them more or less determined to rise up again.

As the beat of the war-drums from Washington grew louder, the funerals in Karbala or Najaf continued as before, with families and friends following the timeless ritual of washing the dead before bringing them to the tombs of the imams. The Wadi Salam cemetery stretches as far as the eye can see, its above-ground tombs resembling an endless, miniature Arab city. To one side is the *amgasel*, the wash-house at which the dead are prepared for burial before the eyes of all. In a ceremony that is intimate and intense, they are stripped naked and scrubbed with soap before being wrapped, first in plastic and then in lengths of white cotton inscribed with lines from the Koran. As friends and relatives wept in grief, Mowafak Kahmal Hussein invited me to witness the washing of his 25-year-old nephew who had died that morning, along with two of his friends, in a traffic accident on the road from Baghdad to Babylon. Their bruised and battered young bodies were removed from the coffins and placed gently on a cement slab next to a big bath. After being soaped, they were sprinkled with a scented powder before their final journey. Back on the roof-rack of a creaking taxi, they were driven into the centre of Najaf to be carried in homage around the tomb of Imam Ali before being brought back to the cemetery for burial at dusk.

It's not just the grief that blurs everything in Iraq. Power and politics overlap in what can best be described as a ethno-religious cauldron. The Sunnis and the Shiites are Muslims of different creeds, but all are tribesmen. While the tribal structure appears to be stronger than religion in the lives of Iraqi Sunnis, the reverse is the case for the Shiites – for them the mosque is the dominant influence. Reporting on the Sunni side of the Iraq equation led me to spend much time in tribal mudhefs, but my search for an understanding of the Shiites required long hours in mosques and in the homes or offices of Shiite imams. Mere reporters are simply not allowed into the presence of the spiritual leader of the Shiites, the Grand Ayatollah Ali al-Sistani, but his deputies and acolytes in Baghdad and across the south of Iraq left me in no doubt as to his pervasive authority, which extends from the mosques through the network of Shiite tribes to inform almost every aspect of the daily life of millions of Shiites. To complicate matters further, some tribes are mixed Sunni and Shiite, a product of moments in history when clans within a tribe saw an advantage in going over to the other side, such as when the Ottoman Empire accepted the Shiite community's claim that its men should not have to join the imperial army.

While the American bureaucrats, the Iraqi exiles who arrived in Baghdad in the first exciting days of liberation and most of the new Iraqi political parties lunged for the institutions of power, the Shiite religious leadership went to the people and the streets and now seem to be better placed politically. The US was confident in its belief that the exiles would form a savvy and suited new governing elite in Baghdad. Instead Washington is now confronted by a robed and bearded near-saint, a formidable opponent who says very little but means what he says. Even if al-Sistani

compromises and accepts a US-sponsored framework for the future political development of Iraq – one that might allow George W. Bush to unfurl
again his "mission accomplished" banner – there are grave fears among
secular Shiites and non-Shiite Iraqis that an al-Sistani dominated regime
might quickly evolve into something very different, perhaps something
very theocratic, maybe something very Iranian.

As the Iraq war approached, I was repeatedly confronted with questions in radio and TV interviews that could only be answered as facts were
progressively revealed on the ground. Some of these imponderables have
now been resolved. Would Iraqi forces put up a fight? – yes, some would,
I thought. How many would die? – thousands. Would a good, hard jab in
the chest cause Saddam and his regime simply to collapse and fade away?
– probably. Would the US find weapons of mass destruction? – probably
not, I wrote. The biggest, most fraught question, though, is still being
answered – how would Iraqis respond to Saddam's demise and to a US
occupation? Could the Americans push and prod them along a fragile
diplomatic path, as they were attempting to do with the people of
Afghanistan, to form what might one day become an acceptable representative government. Or, like Yugoslavia after the death of the dictator
Josef Tito, would Iraq descend into civil war? At least part of this question will be answered in Najaf, where today the city's crumbling walls are
papered with faces from a procession of Saddam Hussein's Shiite victims.
Just as it remembers its ancient dead, the city remembers its recent dead
and it fully understands the implications of their deaths for Iraq's grim
future.

There was always going to be a good deal of sabre-rattling with the
loosening of Saddam's iron grip. We could only guess at the political and
religious torrents that would be unleashed, but within days of the fall of
Baghdad there was blood on the steps of the Najaf mosque. A prominent
and pro-US Shiite activist had been brutally murdered, and at the same
time al-Sistani's home was surrounded by gun-toting young activists
who demanded that he clear out of Najaf within forty-eight hours. The

siege ended only with the arrival of armed Shiite tribal leaders and their fighters who entered the city to protect the Grand Ayatollah.

Freed of Saddam's tyranny, fissures threatened to split the Shiite community as old family rivalries erupted. The murdered activist was Sheikh Abdel Majid al-Khoei, the fifty-year-old head of the London-based philanthropic Khoei Foundation and a son of the late Grand Ayatollah Abdul Kassin al-Khoei. He had been airlifted into Najaf by the Americans as a strong supporter of the US who might dislodge al-Sistani from his position as paramount leader of the Shiite community. Al-Sistani had worried the Americans with his each-way bet in the lead-up to the war. He had issued a *fatwa* to his followers urging them not to fight for Saddam; more troubling for Washington was his parallel edict that neither should Shiites fight for the US. In other words, like him, they should sit on their hands. Also weighing into the struggle for power and recognition in the Shiite world was the Iran-based Supreme Council for Islamic Revolution in Iraq (SCIRI), set up by Ayatollah Muhammad Bakr al-Hakim, son of another Shiite grand ayatollah who first challenged Iraqi secular regimes as far back as the 1950s. Ayatollah al-Hakim followed in his father's steps as an Islamic scholar, but when his father died in the 1970s, the leadership of Iraqi's Shiites was taken up by Mohammed Bakr al-Sadr who encouraged Shiites to join al-Dawa – meaning Islamic Voice – an outlawed militant organisation that opposed Saddam. Saddam retaliated by ordering a brutal crackdown on the Shiite leadership. After an attempt to kill Tariq Aziz, Saddam's deputy, in the 1980s, Mohammed Bakr al-Sadr and his sister were arrested in 1999. She is said to have been raped in front of him, and he is said to have died after nails were driven through his head.

It was at this point that Ayatollah al-Hakim fled to Iran and the protection of the late Ayatollah Khomeini who, before becoming leader of Iran, had been exiled in Najaf. In Iran, Ayatollah al-Hakim set up an exiles' militia that regularly crossed into Iraq and which, in the wake of the 1991 Gulf War, briefly took the southern Iraqi city of Basra. Ayatollah al-Hakim paid a cruel price for his political and militant opposition.

In an interview with *The New Yorker*'s Jon Lee Anderson in Iran early in 2003, he said, "I was burnt with cigarettes, electro-shocked. My head was put into a metal vice. I was beaten very harshly and imprisoned in a cell where I couldn't distinguish between night and day. All of this happened when I was in my youth. When I was an older man, five of my brothers and nine of my nephews were killed. Fifty of my relatives were killed or disappeared. I've had seven assassination attempts against me, but I depend on the Almighty to cleanse my soul, and I am not tired, I will continue." But he "continued" only until August 2003 when his beatific visage went up on the wall poster memorial to Najaf's dead. With eighty-nine others, al-Hakim died in a car-bomb attack outside the mosque that houses Ali's tomb. A banner marks the spot: REVENGE, REVENGE – NO MATTER HOW LONG IT TAKES. And in March 2004, on the holiest day in the Shiite calendar, close to 200 Shiites died in a series of co-ordinated bomb attacks on huge crowds attending commemorations at mosques in Baghdad and Karbala.

In the year since Bush landed his invasion force in Iraq, Najaf has reasserted itself as the spiritual heart of the country. The back-alley office of the Grand Ayatollah al-Sistani has become a serious rival to Baghdad as a seat of political power. To this day the Grand Ayatollah remains an enigma. He has no political party and no army. He rarely speaks his mind and he hardly ever ventures from the ascetic home where he receives few guests – and certainly not Bush's man in Iraq, Paul Bremer.

American Vice-President Dick Cheney and Defense Secretary Donald Rumsfeld are reportedly of the view that al-Sistani can still be stared down, but in June 2003 the grey beard, as old men are affectionately referred to in Iraq, quietly issued a second *fatwa*, insisting on the right of all Iraqis to have a direct say in electing a new government and the team of experts to draft the constitution under which they would live. The Americans made the mistake of concluding that the frail old man of Najaf could be ignored, but late last year Washington buckled, dumping its plans for the political transition. Out went a long-held timetable that the

US, and many others vying for power in the new Iraq, had hoped would give more secular and US-friendly political forces time to take control. In the vacuum left by the toppling of Saddam, the mosque was one of the few remaining threads of the social fabric that survived. Although the powerful dynastic families of the religious sheikhs had been at war for years – and still are – they have proved to be more adept than Washington's Johnnies-come-lately at sensing the political mood.

All the key Shiite sheikhs are clerics. After al-Sistani, the most prominent is Abdul Aziz al-Hakim, a brother of the assassinated Ayatollah al-Hakim, who took over from the dead man as leader of the Supreme Council for Islamic Revolution in Iraq after the August 2003 bombing. Al-Hakim has co-operated with the US, taking a seat on the Washington-appointed Interim Governing Council, the ineffectual 25-man team of mostly exiles set up to put an Iraqi face on the US occupation. Al-Hakim has served as the IGC's rotating chairman, but has embraced the al-Sistani line. Working alongside SCIRI is the Dawa Party, less powerful but similar in its outlook and in its broad support for al-Sistani. They are being eclipsed by the anti-establishment firebrand, Moqutada al-Sadr, whose father once led the al-Dawa movement. This young man refuses to divulge his age – his fat, chubby face puts him anywhere between twenty and thirty – but al-Sadr is the living embodiment of how Iraqi sons inherit the power of their fathers. Al-Sadr tries desperately to fill the shoes of his much-respected father. His age and his lack of scholarship would ordinarily make him a junior player, but as his father's only surviving son he has inherited much of the family's clout and he has turbo-charged his father's view that, as in Iran, Iraq's senior clerics should wield political power. He may have been elbowed from the top table by the mainstream Shiite leadership, but al-Sadr has strong support in the teeming slums of Baghdad and in other pockets of the country. He too embraces the al-Sistani line, but only to the extent that it fits naturally with his virulent anti-American, pro-Iranian rhetoric. I was at one of his press conferences in Najaf when he argued that killing Americans did not constitute terrorism, and later I heard him preach a thinly veiled warning to Iraqis who worked with the Americans that the price of collaboration was death.

The al-Hakim and al-Sadr families vie for more than political power. Each has their own army, and while much of the roiling between them centres on family prestige and honour, a lot also has to do with control of the massive pilgrim donations that pour through the mosques of Najaf and Karbala. Among some Shiites there is a very matter-of-fact debate, which seems to take place with absolutely no sense of outrage, about how long it might be before al-Hakim's militia assassinates Moqutada al-Sadr.

Washington and some Iraqi players believed that al-Sadr could be marginalised, but instead he took control of the impoverished sectors of Baghdad, places like the garbage-strewn maze of Al-Sadr City, named for his father, and Al-Shualla. It was assumed he would confine his political activity to the slums, manipulating the post-Saddam fears and anxieties of the impoverished, the uneducated and the unemployed who, in the early days of the occupation, saw that it was his loyal clerics who imposed security, dealt with looters and restored basic services. Frustration with the stumbling Iraqi political establishment has broadened his following.

The young al-Sadr was pulled to centre stage in March–April 2004 by US decisions to close an al-Sadr newspaper, to detain one of his senior lieutenants and to seek his – al-Sadr's – arrest on a warrant implicating him in the April 2003 murder of Abdul Majid al-Khoei on the steps of the Najaf mosque. The result of these ill-considered actions was an explosion of anti-American resentment that hurled the Shiites into battle, not against the Sunnis or the Kurds but against the US forces. That all of this coincided with the death of hundreds of Iraqis in punishing US attacks on the Sunni stronghold of Falluja served only to intensify Iraqi anger at the occupation of their country. Overnight al-Sadr declared himself to be the "striking arm" in Iraq of the terrorist groups Hamas and Hezbollah, and opinion polls that had previously rated his popularity in low single digits now recorded degrees of support for him in excess of 50 per cent. The Sunni resistance fighters who had previously been seen as isolated pockets of resistance to the inevitable US domination of the country were recast as national heroes. A wave of foreign hostage-taking completed what some commentators called Washington's "perfect storm", a reference to the Sebastian Junger book in which three Atlantic storms collide in an apocalyptic show of nature's force.

After the perfect storm, American intelligence officers quoted by The New York Times contradicted their president, arguing that the US faced a broad-based Shiite uprising that went well beyond supporters of al-Sadr, and that a much larger number of Shiites had turned against the occupation even if they had not played an active part in the uprising. At the time of this essay going to press, al-Sadr was playing a knife-edge game of catch-me-if-you-can with the US military and the rest of the Shiite leadership. Surrounded by his Medhi militia, he had hunkered in Najaf next to the Imam Ali Mosque, which in mid-May 2004 suffered minor combat damage to its golden dome. Al-Sadr's strategy was to attempt to draw US fire in the direction of the shrine or the nearby home of al-Sistani, either of which events would provoke international condemnation. The city's senior clerics had drawn "red lines" around the mosque and other shrines and warned the US and al-Sadr that there was to be no fighting within the lines. There were growing fears that such restraint on the part of the US could spark intra-Shiite fighting as militia forces loyal to al-Sistani were drawn into an attempt to herd al-Sadr's forces towards the main US forces waiting on the outskirts of the city.

The first anniversary of the fall of Baghdad – the weekend of 11 April 2004 – had marked the first time in decades in which Shiites were able to make their annual al-Arbi'een pilgrimage to Karbala. The first six people I interviewed by the roadside, thirty kilometres south of Baghdad, declared unswerving loyalty to al-Sadr. The US siege of Falluja had begun, and an unscientific straw poll I conducted of sixty pilgrims produced a staggering result – support was divided almost evenly between the radical al-Sadr and the enigmatic al-Sistani, but there was virtually no support for the returned Shiite exiles and power-brokers whose new parties are supposed to be the building blocks in the floundering US effort to establish a political democracy in Iraq.

Unquestionably, al-Sistani is the supreme Shiite leader of Iraq. His critique of the American plans for Iraq is not far removed from al-Sadr's, but he is a peaceable and deft politician. Privately, the other Shiite leaders tear al-Sadr to pieces, but to confront him publicly would be political suicide. To criticise his anti-American rant as Iraqis are being killed by Americans would allow them to be portrayed as pro-American – not a good look in today's Iraq.

It is difficult to understand the detailed positions of any of the Shiite leaders – al-Sistani included – because they speak in riddles or not at all. Policies, if they can be called such, are laid down in the most general terms. Yet, as the chaos of the US occupation continues to compare badly with the relative, albeit oppressive, order of day-to-day existence during the Saddam years, the clerics gain power at a greater rate. Under Saddam, the Iranian-born al-Sistani said little. What is not clear is whether his silence at that time was chiefly a way of protecting his followers from more regime-inflicted pain, or whether it embodied a rejection of the insistence of his fundamentalist Iranian counterparts that the most scholarly clerics, like him, should oversee key aspects of government. Likewise, it is only apparent – as opposed to clearly articulated – that he is now intervening so directly in the political process because of the prize of control that Shiites see within their grasp; he may be equally or more concerned with the economic and social suffering of his people as the Americans try to impose order. There is much second guessing – as much by the Americans as by Iraqis.

The influence that al-Sistani commands over most Shiite leaders makes it impossible for the Americans to go behind his back. The leaders of the various Shiite political parties have openly acknowledged that they would not act in concert with the US without first consulting the Grand Ayatollah. The Americans can use the other Shiite leaders as messengers, but ultimately al-Sistani will make or break their Iraqi democracy. Given the swirling mix of tribal and mosque power, what emerges at the end of this process is unlikely to resemble anything that Washington had in mind when it embarked on its project of regime change.

The controversial interim constitution drafted by the US provided a massive security blanket for the three Kurdish provinces in the far north of the country. This has proved the most crucial stumbling block to gaining Shiite support for the constitution. As written, the clause allows a two-thirds vote in any of the three provinces (such as the near-autonomous Kurdistan) to immediately force a new election next year by vetoing the permanent constitution that must be drafted by the new legislature. This, say the Shiites, is inordinate power for the Kurdish community, which comprises less than a million people in a population of 25 million. The Shiites also oppose what they see as a bid to bind next year's elected assembly, which they are likely to dominate, through a clause in the interim document that bars any changes to the constitution without the approval of three-quarters of the elected parliament and a consensus endorsement by the proposed president and his two deputies, at least one of whom will not be Shiite. Another issue which was fudged in the constitution, but which is likely to be crisis-making for the new government, is Islamic law. Some Shiites want sharia to accompany the declaration of Islam as the official religion of Iraq, but Islamic law is cited merely as "a source" for legislation, creating the potential for an argument that this is not enough or that it gives non-elected religious leaders too much power to intervene in the parliament. Yet another issue is the rights of women. The constitution says that 25 per cent of the elected parliament must be women, but in a region where their rights often are ignored, it is vague or silent on equal rights in marriage, inheritance and the citizenship of children.

When I interviewed Said Kamal Adine al-Mukudas al-Kurfi, one of al-Sistani's representatives in Baghdad and a senior member of the five-man Hawza committee over which al-Sistani presides, he dismissed the

Sunnis as "only 20 percent of Iraq", telling me, "If al-Sistani says anything, all the political parties will respect him." Swathed in brown robes and sitting on the cushioned floor of his home in the inner Baghdad suburb of Hikarama, he said with a finality that would have winded those who believe in some kind of Sunni–Shiite rapprochement after the battle of Falluja, "The Sunnis have ruled Iraq for too long. The new government will be Shiite." Then he seemed to lecture Washington on the rudiments of democracy: "It's like Britain and the US – the majority vote wins ... and if Washington doesn't like that, what can they do?" Without stating this explicitly, he introduced an Iranian analogy into our debate: "Al-Sistani will see the written constitution before he endorses it, but he is big enough and powerful enough to reject it. And whoever is the president of the Iraqi Governing Council needs to keep going to al-Sistani to get his permission for what the council is doing." Producing a comb with which to rake his flowing white beard, he shed only a glimmer of light on al-Sistani's thinking: "I have spoken to him about the government we will have, and he said that the most important thing is not about being 100 per cent like Iran, so much as having safety and security for the people of Iraq." The power had failed again, but a beam of sunlight fought its way through the shutters, setting ablaze the red stone in a ring on his finger as he assessed the performance of the US administration: "The US came as liberators, but they have become occupiers. They promised us a good life – democracy and freedom. But look at how we live. We don't have electricity or telephones or benzene or cooking gas or security. And people are being killed in the streets. Now you tell me, is that clever or stupid?"

In Najaf, Abud Zaid al-Jabari was on a floor cushion too, sitting behind a cut-down desk from which he runs the Najaf branch of Abdul Aziz al-Hakim's Supreme Council for Islamic Revolution in Iraq. The officials of the former regime wore Saddam watches; the face of his timepiece bore the image of a Shiite holy man. Al-Jabari was reluctant to name countries that might be emulated by what will be the first Arab Shiite regime beyond the postage-stamp emirate of Bahrain, telling me only, "Not everything in Iran is right and the Turks have made mistakes. So we have to take some of the good things from Iran and from Turkey and from other countries." Asked about the role of al-Sistani, he said simply, "Al-Sistani is my opinion – we wait for who and what he chooses. Yes, he is so supreme that he does not have to be elected and he does have a power of veto. All Iraqi people respect the religious scholars and they say yes to what the scholars decide." Asked why al-Sistani remained so Delphic in the absence of Saddam, he said, "The Grand Ayatollah is still afraid to use all his power, even though Saddam is gone. But if he doesn't agree with the new constitution, the people of Iraq will never agree to it." Searching for a Western equivalent, he suggested, "Al-Sistani is our version of the Pope." When I suggested that millions of Roman Catholics did not adhere to the word of John Paul II in its entirety, he seemed surprised and countered, "If al-Sistani calls for the people of Iraq to die, they are ready." He too initiated a comparison with the strong-arm role of clerics in Iran, when he argued that whatever the nature of the new Iraqi government, there would have to be a supervisory council of "people with good personal histories and knowledge of politics" to oversee its work. He then outlined his party's policy on women. They could vote and work, but they would never enjoy the freedom that women in the West enjoy: "Our women are different. We have to protect their bodies and dressing like women in the West is not freedom." Alcohol? It would not be tolerated. But time was up, and we had not yet addressed the more contentious issue of justice. When the clerics insist on justice, as they frequently do, it often means traditional Islamic law, much of which is at odds with Western justice.

In Baghdad's Alawi quarter, I found the Shiite imam, Sheikh Mohammed Hussein al-Kinana, a small mosque preacher with strong views. The only picture that could be seen in his home was a portrait of the fundamentalist Iranian Ayatollah Khomeini. He too put only the lightest brush-strokes on his picture of the new Iraq: "A democracy without extremists. We are not like the Iranians – we don't want to chop off the hands of looters." Women's rights? "No law in the world is better than Islam in its protection of women." Kirkuk for the Kurds? "No … they have wanted it for a long time, but they can't have it." What of the role of al-Sistani? Tucking his legs under his bottom on the hard wooden bench on which he sat, he argued, "Al-Sistani is not Khomeini, but people will do as he says because his legitimacy comes from Islam. After we have an elected government, he will guide us only on spiritual issues." Tell him that the people didn't elect al-Sistani, and his rejoinder comes as quick as a flash: "They didn't elect Bremer's Iraqi Governing Council either." Reminded that many in the West saw Ayatollah Khomeini as an extremist, he replied matter-of-factly, "That is only because people in the West do not understand Khomeini."

How does the US stop a new Iraqi regime from spiralling into a pale imitation of the charades of democracy – or its total absence – in so many Muslim countries? How much more religion will Washington accept than there is in, say, Turkey? How much less democracy than there is in Iran? The difficulty facing Bush and Bremer is they don't know how far they can push al-Sistani before the Ayatollah urges Shiites to line up with the Sunnis against the US occupation.

Some in the American administration cling to a hope that divisions within the Shiite community might allow the Pentagon's favourite exile, the discredited Ahmed Chalabi, a secular Shiite, to march through the middle of the field to lead a new government – but even he fell out spectacularly with Washington in May 2004. Failing that, they are putting the best possible gloss on whatever al-Sistani might guide into place – what they perceive as his need to do the best for Shiites while doing enough for Kurds and Sunnis for the sake of national unity, along with their conclusion that enough of the Shiite clerical and political leadership has spent sufficient time in Iran to know that the road to Tehran is not the way to the future. Although Iraq will not necessarily become a cleric-driven new Iran, al-Sistani is already well entrenched as a Khomeini-type figure who offers himself as a revered friend and protector of all citizens, just as Khomeini and Saddam did on the road to power and for which they were warmly embraced by the people of their respective countries. For now there is only a shaky consensus about what al-Sistani is not. The tea-leaf readers presume he does not want a Khomeini theocracy, but he is yet to reveal precisely where he might seek to position Iraq on the tenuous democratic yardstick that runs from Ankara to Tehran.

The Shiite leaders are adept at making soothing pronouncements, sticking to generalities and motherhood statements in the hope that they can take control of Iraq by apparent consensus. However, in an un-guarded moment, a prominent Shiite cleric, Grand Ayatollah Mohammad Taqi al-Modaresi, warned that the interim constitution – as written – was "a time bomb that will spark a civil war in Iraq if it goes off".

The man most likely to be Iraq's first Shiite president, the bespec-tacled and scholarly looking Abdul Aziz al-Hakim, has taken over the block-house, riverfront mansion that was home to Tariq Aziz, who now languishes in a US-run prison. When I arrived, members of his black-clad Bard Brigade militia were engaged in target practice, shooting pigeons on a huge concrete bridge that overshadows the house as it sets out to span the Tigris River.

One of al-Hakim's key advisers is Dr Hamid al-Bayati, a recently returned exile who was a key link between the Shiites and foreign gov-ernments from his base in exile in London. In an interview he put a little more meat on the bones of a prospective Iraqi democracy: "We have to take Iraqi reality into account. We can't copy any one democratic system in the world and apply it here." But, unlike some, he was not shy about stating what to Shiites is obvious: "I have to be frank and say that all the Iraqi minorities are worried about the Shiites having a majority, especial-ly the Sunnis. But this is the reality and we can't change the make-up of the Iraqi people. It's obvious that the Shiite majority of the people will elect a Shiite majority in the assembly. They have tried to provoke us with the attack that killed our former leader and then with the 2 March attacks on our most emotional holy day. But so far we have not responded. We realise there is a conspiracy to provoke a civil war between the Sunnis and us. But it's not just up to the Shiites. It's up to all in the community to stop the push for war."

Much of the talk can be dismissed as rhetoric: it conforms with the lurid exaggerations that sometimes shock newcomers to the Middle East, but which often cause the eyes of more experienced observers to glaze over. Yet the rise in sectarian violence in liberated Iraq is deeply troubling proof that when the Americans pull back, the idea that "mine enemy's enemy is my friend" will count for little.

SNAPSHOTS

No matter where I went in Iraq, including in Baghdad, tribal and religious politics invariably informed what people told me about their life and country before and after the US-led invasion. The educated and business elite of Baghdad tends to be disdainful of the tribes and the mosques, but listening to Iraqi policemen plead impotence in the face of the intervention of the sheikhs – tribal and religious – in their efforts to impose law and order; and hearing countless tales of the resort to tribal justice or to the unofficial mosque-run courts established in the post-invasion vacuum, I was left with a sense that this was a power too great to be swept aside by the American intruders.

The Police

Capt Hassam, a cop without a pistol who wears a uniform he bought himself, was full of despondency and anecdotes to back it up. Lighting up another cigarette, he said, "We can't tell a tribal sheikh or a mosque imam what to do – they tell us what to do." He made his point by telling the story of a clash in the Baghdad suburbs. As an Iraqi policemen fired shots in the air to disperse a crowd, he was joined by US forces whose gunfire killed one of the protesters. "The sheikh of the dead man's tribe decided that the Iraqi policeman had killed him and demanded that he must pay tribal compensation for the death … if he doesn't the tribe will mount a revenge killing against him. This is why so many Iraqi police sit in their homes instead of going to work. I say that maybe 35 per cent of all the new policemen have quit. And for some Iraqi police and soldiers, it's easier to go and fight with the resistance against the Americans than to stay in the police and the army and fight Iraqis."

Later on the same day I had tea with two Shiite soldiers from the Iraq Civil Defense Corps (ICDC) who insisted that professionalism was foremost, until I asked if they would accept orders to fight alongside the US against the Sunni insurgents in Falluja or the Shiite fighters at Najaf.

In other words, would they kill Iraqis? "Oh, we wouldn't be asked," one of them parried. What did they think of others refusing to go to the frontline? "That's their decision."

Were they discomforted by the news from Falluja? Pause. There was much debate between them in Arabic before one came back lamely: "We need more time to think about this …" But surely this was a hot topic of discussion in the ranks? "No. We don't discuss it." Finally they thought they had me in a corner. The fighting had died down at Falluja, where the targets would have been Sunnis, but US forces were now massing for a possible attack on Najaf, where their guns would be pointed at their fellow Shiites. I wondered if they would obey orders to go to Najaf. "If the Americans attack Najaf, come back and ask me," one of them said, and the other chimed in, too quickly, "That's an intelligent answer, isn't it?"

In what must be seen as a belated admission that it was a mistake to disband Saddam's military and security apparatus, the US has begun a process of hand-picking former members and installing them to toughen up the new security forces. Even so, it is widely expected that when there is a crisis after 30 June, individual members will revert to the allegiances and practices of their tribal or religious origins. As it stands, the police are subjected to ritualistic humiliation. There is a widespread lack of confidence in their investigative skills and a total refusal by city motorists and others to acknowledge their authority. It's difficult for a new police force to command respect when the principal of tha'r spreads the tribal responsibility to exact revenge as widely across a generation as a forty-second cousin of the victim; or as deeply through the generations as his grandchildren.

In some Baghdad suburbs, such as Adhamiya, Shiite residents are voting with their weapons and feet on the issue of police confidence and setting up vigilante gangs to pursue Sunnis whom they suspect of participating in violence. Likewise with Salaam my translator, who volunteered over dinner at his home the fact that he had reverted to tribal form when he became anxious about strangers arriving in his predominantly Shiite neighbourhood: "The police? I went to the imam at the Sunni mosque and I warned him – he would die if any Wahabis came into our area. I told him my family [read "tribe"], is big and we would deal with him."

It was the same out in the Ramadi desert, where they were mourning the death of Sheikh Malik. An expert on tribal culture and politics warned me, "If the family doesn't take revenge against the US, it will lose face. The tribe is going to pick up a very high-ranking American as revenge for Malik's death; then there will be lots of others to make up for the other members of his family who died in the bombing."

Like other guerrilla conflicts, Iraq has become a war of attrition. The measures taken by the Americans to protect themselves make the US forces a difficult target, so the insurgents turn instead on Iraqis who are seen to be helping the US – police and other security workers, the judiciary and local political leaders. The insurgents have made a special project of threatening and assassinating Iraqi translators, who are a vital link between outsiders and the local population.

Collaborators

The translators' courage is matched only by their naivety. In the interpreters' shack at the US base in Adhamiya, three young Iraqis spoke fondly – in newly Americanised English – of their new employers and expressed their hopes about what the US might do for Iraq. They were aiming much higher than Starbucks and McDonalds. Omar al-Captain, twenty-one, wanted Microsoft to open in Baghdad and he wanted an American college there, just like the ones in Cairo and Beirut. Saif Ahmed, twenty-three, hankered for the American justice system, and Mohammed Suphi, twenty-three, hoped that Baghdad would one day have theatres and amusement arcades like they have in New York.

They may not live to see their dreams realised. Post-war Iraq is a bitter place, and the decision by these three to accept the occupying Americans' money is seen by many as an act of treachery. Chillingly, they have been told that they are being targeted as collaborators. Al-Captain has been named on an anonymous death-list that has been handed out around local mosques. When I first interviewed him in the autumn of 2003, he was No. 2 on the list, a personal copy of which was slipped under the door of his family home. When I returned in the spring of 2004, he was in hiding ... and nursing his wounds after a gun attack which he managed to survive. He slept in a different house each night and kept his hand close to a pistol given to him by an American officer. He carried a frayed copy of the death-list in his wallet, with a circle around the names of those who have been attacked. Already three of these are dead and another three have been cowed into quitting a job that requires them to accompany the US raiding parties that seek out members of the resistance and the remnants of Saddam's regime.

A few weeks before we met, Suphi was returning to his home after working a shift that ended at 9 p.m. He said, "There was a commotion at a nearby restaurant and I saw the US military vehicles. The body of a man was on the ground. There was a pool of blood under his head. It was our colleague Omeed Luay. He was shot in the back of the head by a gunman who yelled 'Traitor! Traitor!'" A second man on the list died in a rocket-propelled grenade attack on a US convoy, and a third was decapitated in a knife attack in the back streets of Adhamiya. Another on the list survived a grenade attack on his home, and a journalist who had written that Iraqis should follow the Kuwaiti example of working with the Americans cheated death when his home was sprayed with gunfire. All three of the young men I spoke to said that they had taken to lying about their new work, telling neighbours that they are working in shops or businesses that are some distance from their homes.

Despite the danger – or because of it – they seemed to be on a high as they talked about their work. Al-Captain, in particular, was obviously exhilarated as the darkened Humvees raced out on night patrol, his legs dangling over the side and his head swathed in a mask that made him look like a player in one of the Hollywood thrillers they all enjoy – even in Saddam's time Baghdad's Ali Baba market was flooded with bootleg videos and DVDs. By day the translators insist on going about their normal lives, attending college, seeing girlfriends. There is little the US can do to protect them. Ahmed: "The issue of protection is for us to decide. We don't have to do this work. I was frightened after the death of Omeed Luay. I thought about quitting, I could see it happening to me. But I believe in what we are doing. Besides, I need the money to fund my studies. People in the streets yell at us, calling us US dogs and CIA spies. When we talk to Iraqis in the houses that are raided, some of them warn us in Arabic that we will die soon."

The risk is heightened because the job makes them ambassadors for the US. They plead for patience from neighbours who are upset about power and water supplies; under the US, these have been much more unreliable than under Saddam. Al-Captain: "In the thirty-five years that he ruled, Saddam poisoned Iraqis about the US. The Americans have been here for only four months. Somehow, we have to get to a point five years from now and then look back. The Kuwaitis worked with the US for thirteen years to fix their war damage. They are still working on it, so we have to be patient." Ahmed: "There are more important things than McDonalds and Chevrolets. I want to see freedom – people here are still so afraid to say anything against Saddam that they have not thought about the meaning of liberty." Suphi: "I'm waiting for the day we can walk in the streets and tell our neighbours that we are interpreters for the US without getting killed." For now they dream. Al-Captain wants to study political science at Columbia University, to travel in the US and France and to work as a United Nations peace-keeper. Suphi wants to study computer science in the US and to visit Las Vegas. Ahmed wants to visit Italy – "to see a real game of soccer".

Reprisals

Al-Gharaf is a market town about thirty kilometres from the predomi-nantly Shiite city of Nassiriya, in the south of Iraq. I had come here to see Aziz Abass A'aileykh. At his home on the edge of the town, I received a traditional welcome. One of his sons brought a communal water bowl, which was followed by small glasses of sweet tea before A'aileykh insisted on serving a breakfast of Iraqi bread with fresh cream and tinned cheese. He was an old-guard Baathist who had quit the party early in Saddam's rise to power. Now he had adapted to a new climate of fear in Iraq: where portraits of Saddam once appeared in his home, there are posters of Islamic holy men. "They're for protection – you still can't speak your mind in this country," he said gravely. Sitting cross-legged on the rich reds and blues of carpets that were the only relief from the raw cement finish of his home, he addressed me as "Habibi ...", which means "My friend ..."

"People want money as compensation for those who were executed or jailed by Saddam's regime. The families of the victims are threatening the members of Saddam's execution squads," he said. "They even make demands on the widows of Baathist officials who have been dead for years. The price is three million to five million Iraqi dinars ($US2000 to $US3300), even more – it depends on the power of their tribe. Sometimes it's a bullet in the head; sometimes a grenade in their homes. A lot of my old friends have returned to their tribal lands, seeking the protection of their sheikhs. If people intend to kill them, they would not dare when they are with the sheikhs because it would mean inter-tribal war."

The temperature was in the high-fifties – Celsius – and as a broiling breeze caused the lace curtains on an opening in the wall to billow till they bunched, Aziz Abass A'aileykh revealed that a cousin who had been a member of the provincial council of the Baath Party was hiding nearby. After some discussion of the security issues involved, he agreed to fetch his cousin to speak for himself. It would take some time to bring him, and cushions were brought so that I could sleep through the worst of the midday heat. Two hours later A'aileykh returned with the stubble-faced Ali Kamal. In his sixties, he had heavy-framed, thick glasses; he wore a traditional white dishdasha and, despite the heat, a braid-edged cloak of wool so fine that it was almost transparent. He had been persuaded to come by his cousin, but it was evident that he was uneasy. Kamal was what you'd expect from an active Baathist – hard. He still had the bearing of a man accustomed to power, but a hunted look came into his eyes as he refused to name the village in which he hid: "There is no reason to tell you … except to say it is the village in which I was born and it belongs to my tribe."

The regime did appalling things to people in this area, but Kamal swore that he had done nothing wrong: "I was just an ordinary party member." He sharply dismissed deserters from Saddam's army as criminals and he justified execution as the "fate of oppositionists all over the world". He chose not to understand a question about how those who had done the hunting under Saddam had become the hunted after his demise, but he matter-of-factly explained how he and his family had rapidly fallen from grace with the demise of the former regime: "We knew they would want to kill us because in 1991 they went after the Baathists in the Shiite uprising after the Kuwait war. As the Americans came into Nassiriya we were instructed by the leadership to swap our party uniforms for dishdashas and to get out of town fast. I had to leave everything – my two houses and my Baath Party car. We just drove away to be with our relatives and tribes in country, where no one can touch us." He became maudlin, complaining about the risk and disruption for his adult children and their families, but when I asked how it felt to be on the lam, he came back with all the bombast of the party official: "I can go back to my Nassiriya houses any time I like." His cousin A'aileykh observed dryly, "Yes, and if you do, you will die a quick death."

The next morning my translator hailed a taxi to take us to the al-Salihia slum quarter, where the unpaved streets were deep with garbage and the butcher's shop was a steel post stuck in the ground, on which he had hung a sheep carcass which he was selling, bit by bit. We soon found what we were looking for, the home of 28-year-old Gasaq Talib. He hesitated before inviting us in to talk about his 53-year-old father, whose murderers had pursued him all the way to the shrine city of Karbala. There was a family discussion and finally the story came out. "A group of men captured him at the Al-Huer shrine. They took him to the Al-Razaza Highway where they tied his hands and used his *kaffiyeh* to gag him before they put three pistol shots in the back of his head. He worked full-time for the Baath Party. We know that is why they killed him, because they did not rob him. If he was evil we would settle according to tribal justice, but he was a peaceful man. Now we have fourteen children to feed in this house and they will not give us his pension. People say they will not employ me or my brother because we are our father's sons. The ones who killed him 'killed' three others – my grandmother has not been able to get out of her bed since my father's death, my grandfather has become senile and my mother has had a breakdown. But we can't seek revenge because we don't know his killers."

Insurgents

I had several clandestine meetings with fighters in the insurgency, chief among them Ahmed, a weapons dealer and insurgency group commander, and Haqi, one of his foot soldiers. Our second meeting took place in the garden of the comfortable home of one of his relatives in a west Baghdad suburb, where the black shadows of women glide through the streets at dusk with colourfully dressed children trailing behind. The warm night air was so heavy that when Ahmed exhaled, his cigarette smoke hung just where he parked it. Ahmed denied having served in Saddam's military or in any of his security agencies. He offered a peculiar account of how he had avoided military service: "I put lots of tea leaves in cold water and gulped it down so that it filled my lungs. The tea showed up as spots in my lungs and after I paid the doctor some money, I was rejected on health grounds." Why then had he signed up for the resistance after going to such lengths to avoid serving Saddam? He replied, "Saddam was a loser. His wars were useless and he made enemies of our Muslim neighbours."

This weapons dealer was uncomfortable talking about war in a family environment, so he made a satellite phone call, organising the use of a room in a nondescript hotel nearer to the city. Its ground-floor windows and all but one of its doors were still bricked up to fend off looters. Slightly more at ease, Ahmed sat in a formal armchair at the hotel, the folds of his white *dishdasha* draped over its red brocade upholstery. Toying with his close-cut beard, he described a disciplined and religiously focused Sunni resistance. Asked where authority rested, he said, "It's with the sheikhs in the mosques. Baath Party people and former members of the military are not allowed to be our leaders. Baathists are losers too – they didn't succeed when they worked for the party. We now have a single, jihadist leadership group that operates nationally. Everything is done on instructions carried by messengers. There are thirty-five men in my cell and I'm a leader of three other cells. The number of foreigners who are coming to help us is increasing – Syrian, Palestinian, Saudi and Qatari. US claims about al-Qaeda and Ansar al-Islam are just propaganda." Going on in Arabic, a language which is as guttural as it is poetic, he told me through a translator, "Our fighters are protecting our religion. We cannot allow foreigners to occupy our country. We suffered under Saddam and we hate him, but we would put him in our hearts ahead of a Christian or a Jew, because he is a Muslim. The Americans do not respect us, so we cannot respect them. They are a cancer of bad things – prostitution, gambling and drugs." His sidekick Haqi butted in at this point: "This struggle is not about Saddam. It's about our country and our God. Our aim is not to have power or to rule the country. We just want the US out and for the word of Allah to be the power in Iraq."

This pocket of the resistance calls itself the Army of Right. Like others, including the Army of Mohammed and the White Flags, it first came to notice in leaflets and graffiti around the Abu Hanifa mosque in Baghdad's predominantly Sunni Adhamiya district.

Both Ahmed, a 32-year-old who has inherited family wealth, including a factory, a farm and a chicken plant, and Haqi refused to give their real names or any information about where they lived. "Iraq is my home," Ahmed said. However, their chat was peppered with references to life on the land and a tribal background. Ahmed reminisced about fishing Iraqi-style as a child. They would drop explosives into the Euphrates to stun fish, which he and his mates would then gather from the river's murky surface; and he had learned how to conceal weapons in his clothing from the sheep smugglers who criss-cross the Jordan–Iraq border.

Ahmed's first mission was an attack on a small US convoy near Balad, in the Tikrit region, three months after the fall of Baghdad. Weeks later he was part of a failed attempt to down a US helicopter at Mahmoudiya, twenty-five kilometres southeast of the capital. He assumed a confident tone as he spoke of the missions: "First we watch the Americans to understand their movements. We know from the way they shoot in every direction that they are afraid." They said that usually the cells operated teams of four or five, two to manage the rocket-propelled grenade launcher and two or three to give covering fire. In most cases, the identity of each fighter was withheld from the others. These resistance fighters relied on tribal networks for information on the Americans and for help to get away in a hurry after an attack. Ahmed explained: "The people offer us hiding places when we are in danger. They support us with words and blessings and sometimes they hide our fighters in the boots of their cars to take them to safety."

Months later, members of a different insurgency group confided their greatest worry to me – the US helicopters. Only their eyes could be seen through a slit in their *keffiyeh* scarves, but there was no mistaking their fear of the black shadows that thunder low overhead, bristling with missiles, guns and surveillance gear. Isam – a *nom de guerre* – spoke with a respect conditioned by experience, although he couldn't help bragging at the same time: "If the choppers weren't flying, the Americans wouldn't last a day in Iraq. They can't fight on the ground – their soldiers are babies; they have powerful weapons but they are scared of us." It was about 9 p.m. when Isam, a 32-year-old teacher, and "Ali", a 28-year-old student, came to a meeting in a private home in one of Baghdad's far-flung suburbs. The meeting had been organised at my request by a third party.

Ali, mostly silent, brandished a German-made MP-5 sub-machinegun, the kind developed for the US Navy, which he said he had stolen from an American soldier. Isam – talkative, excitable and at times weepy – carried a Kalashnikov, which he stood on the floor between his legs, barrel to the ceiling. They belonged to a local cell of between fifty and sixty-five Sunni fighters, based in Ramadi. They seemed genuinely pleased that Saddam Hussein had been arrested forty-eight hours earlier. "We were happy with the fall of the regime. We never cared about Saddam. We are Iraqi citizens and we are fighting for our country," Isam declared with passion. In one of his rare contributions, Ali staked out a religious justification for the insurgency: "The Koran says our land should not be occupied; under Islam we can kill to defend it." Isam outlined the structure of the cell. About fifteen of its members could be described as former Baathists, but none were from Saddam's secret service; they were trained by former Iraqi military officers, but their leader was a rich, thirty-something businessman who funded operations from his own pocket. Individual members – taxi drivers, carpenters, businessmen and farmers – knew only a handful of others in the group, which operated mostly in al-Anbar province, centred on Ramadi. But they also had taken part in attacks on the US in Baghdad and other cities and towns. In more than fifteen attacks, they had operated missile launchers and fired rocket-propelled grenades. "We cleaned out Saddam's military warehouses at Abu Ghraib and Al-Hasiwa. We store the weapons in private homes and we use garbage trucks and ambulances to move them around. We also steal Iraqi police cars and uniforms when we need them. We even use donkey carts – whatever it takes. And if the Americans capture us, we will kill them and ourselves with the body-bombs we wear when we go on the attack." They spoke harshly about Saddam, but Isam reserved his greatest anger for those in the insurgency who organise suicide-bomb attacks on Iraqis rather than Americans. He said, "These attacks make my blood boil.

I swear they are done by the foreign fighters who don't mind destroying our country as they fight the Americans. Why do they kill Iraqi policemen when they could be killing Americans?"

It was when I asked about tribal revenge that Isam cried. He had fought in Saddam's army against the US invasion, but while he did not seek retribution for the death of as many as thirty of his military colleagues during the invasion, he was bent on avenging the death of his two brothers, who had died as resistance fighters in a skirmish with US forces at Falluja. "Between them, they had nine children. I will never forget them, and that is why I'll fight till the last blood."

Pride and shame

For the tribes, pride and shame are issues of great importance. They help to shape communal feeling and determine the workings of law. For individuals, pride and shame have a more directly emotional significance, and this too needs to be grasped if one is to understand the depth of the devastating anger and the increase in anti-American sentiment among Iraqis in the wake of the May 2004 revelations of the American abuse of Iraqi prisoners at Abu Ghraib.

I first encountered the question of shame in the southern desert, when I met with Sheikh Ali Bin Mohammed al-Menshed of the al-Rizi tribe. He invited me to sit with him for the daily gathering in his mudhef – in this case a huge, open-sided Bedouin tent – as he dispensed justice and favours. The thorniest issue of the day concerned the complaint of a Syrian who had stumbled into the mudhef the previous evening, claiming that members of the tribe had stolen his truck and its cargo. Now, after a breakfast of bread, fried liver and thick buffalo cream, the sheikh sat cross-legged before his petitioners. The Syrian was deeply troubled, the reason for which was contained in a letter he produced from his employer – his home was to be confiscated in the event of the truck being "lost". Overnight, however, the truck had been found, after a search of the nearby villages by Sheikh Ali's guards. The head of the tribal clan to which the suspected thieves belonged was summoned. He sat two paces to the right of Sheikh Ali, complaining that he did not command sufficient respect to be able to retrieve the truck from the thieves in his midst. He was met with unbridled rage, as the sheikh exploded: "What am I to do, dismiss you and your family from our territory? I have a punishment worse than death for these thieves of yours! I know their names, and if the truck is not back in forty-eight hours, I will have the men arrested in front of their women and we will make the women come and watch as we hand the men over to the Americans!" I was informed repeatedly that shame in the eyes of women was a greater punishment for male Iraqis than death. An old man sitting beside me in the *mudhef* jolted upright when he heard the sheikh's threat, muttering in Arabic: "Shameful; so dishonourable!"

Shame and its consequences in America's occupation of Iraq were never more eloquently expressed than in a speech made to *The New York Review of Books*' Mark Danner – at about the same time as I was in the south of Iraq at Sheikh Ali's *mudhef* – by a frustrated young man in Falluja: "For Fallujans it is a *shame* to have foreigners break down their doors. It is a *shame* for them to have foreigners stop and search their women. It is a *shame* for the foreigners to put a bag over their heads, to make a man lie on the ground with your shoe on his neck. This is a great *shame*, you understand? This is a great *shame* for the whole tribe. It is the *duty* of that man, and of that tribe, to get revenge on this soldier – to kill that man. Their duty is to attack them, to *wash the shame*. The shame is a *stain*, a dirty thing; they have to *wash* it. No sleep – we cannot sleep until we have revenge. They have to kill soldiers."

The number of Iraqis who have been injured, killed or detained by the Americans can be counted in the tens of thousands. The thought of all of their families, clans and tribes seeking revenge is by itself surely enough to vanquish any hope of an American-imposed democracy taking root in Iraq.

It was evening in Baghdad. In the sitting room of his home, the political scientist Wamidh Nadhmi had just given me a quick history lesson on the topic of the Iraqi tribes. Now he demanded an answer to his own question, the same question on the lips of so many educated Iraqis: "Why don't the Americans simply demand that the sheikhs provide law and order?" Later, Dr Abdul Hamid al-Rawi, from the College of Political Science at the University of Baghdad, came at the same issue from a different angle. As we sipped Pepsi in his high-walled garden, he presented the tribes as the paramount force in Iraq: "As long as a tribe is big and powerful, then its sheikh is big and powerful. Despite the efforts of the British, and the monarchy they installed, and the renegades who plotted against the monarchy and its successor republics, the tribes still exist. If the US works with the tribes in the right way, they might succeed. The tribes could provide security and protection for local directorates, hospitals, schools and factories. They would provide stability and be a dependable ally for the US. This is what the British did in the 1920s. They supported Sheikh Abdul Razak Ali Sulieman. He was the Sheikh of Sheikhs of the Dulame tribe and they gave him the authority of a governor over the western region of Iraq."

All of this raises a fundamental question. If brought into the circle of power, could today's sheikhs stop the attacks on the US? Dr Abdul Hamid certainly believes so, and even given the level of anti-American violence, his explanation resonated with what others had explained to me about the culture of the tribes. "Of course – if there was a deal between the US and the sheikhs to serve Iraq. The sheikhs have the power to declare that there will be no more attacks on the Americans," he said. Could a sheikh control local democratic votes? "But, of course!" Hamid declared emphatically, banging his drink on the table to make his point. "If the US is serious in wanting good relations with the Iraqi people, then it must have good relations with the sheikhs. It is my considered view that loyalty to the tribes is bigger than any ethnic or religious loyalty in Iraq. And since the fall of Baghdad the tribes and tribal law have become even stronger because of the political vacuum. There is no direction or security for the people and they have no one to follow except the tribe and their sheikh."

Adnan Abu Odeh, a former adviser to the late King Hussein of Jordan, argued that the tribes are the strongest social force in what he calls the "broken shell" of the state of Iraq. But, he warned, the sheikhs don't have ambitions beyond their tribes – they are not nationalist in their outlook. In an interview at his home in Amman, he told me that, "The sheikhs know that in the end they'll not be the main game, so they have to benefit as much as possible before the rules change. Probably the most today's sheikh can hope to get is to have as many people from his tribe in the new establishment to sustain benefits for the whole tribe at the highest level possible. Perhaps the sheikhs don't have the power to stop the resistance totally, but they certainly could impede its development by convincing their own tribesmen that it's a losing strategy, or they could be bribed to capture or betray members of the resistance to the US." Other observers made similar assessments of al-Sistani and other senior imams, claiming that they had the power to prod or cajole the Shiite tribes in similar ways. They also contended that the Iraqi Shiite sheikhs were more likely to focus on the spiritual aspects of life, echoing the material–spiritual division between the tribal House of Saud and the Wahabi clerics in Saudi Arabia.

Another former adviser to Jordan's late king is Ali Shukri. Now a member of Saint Anthony's College at Oxford, he spoke to me over Turkish coffee on the grand terrace of Amman's Four Seasons Hotel. "The tribes will listen to anyone who is dishing out money and they can control the level of the resistance, so they can be pillars of the new Iraq. If the US cannot impose law and order, then only the tribes will be able to do it. The Americans might have come across oceans with their Apache helicopters and Bradley fighting vehicles, but if you don't have the support of the tribes in these parts, you are dead. There are two ways to control them. One way is to do just that – by continually attacking and killing them. But if you want them on your side, what will you give them? What's in it for them? Ask them to police the borders and they will do it; they will stop anyone coming into the country. They will name a price. If it is met, they will be on your side. To the extent that the tribes are co-operating with the US right now, it is merely a marriage of convenience. They could be doing a lot more. Overnight, they could give the Americans security, but they will want money, weapons and vehicles to do the job."

Observing all of this from the sidelines is Shariff Ali. More a prince than a sheikh, he is the man who would be king of the new Iraq. Today he operates from what was an official guesthouse of the old regime in the shadow of Baghdad's Babylon Hotel. His supporters commandeered it as a monarchist headquarters after the fall of the capital in April 2003. Dusted-off portraits of banished kings and princes – strained and stuffy – now hang in a marbled lobby that buzzes as servants in *dishdashas* and impressive full-dress bandoliers glide across the shiny floors, serving coffee and water to a predominantly Western-dressed crowd. Shariff Ali, who was two years old when his cousin King Faisal II of Iraq was murdered in 1958, looks and sounds like a product of his exiled British upbringing. After an absence of decades from Iraq, he sat erect in the corner of an ornate sofa and talked of the past and the future: "Tribalism is in our culture; even the urban populations adhere to its customs – hospitality and generosity, honour and honesty. And Saddam's assaults on the institutions of society made people seek the protection and assistance of their tribes, especially as Western sanctions bit through the 1990s. In the harsh post-war environment in which there was no law and order, and no social safety net, people saw themselves not as Iraqis but as members of their tribes. I think the US was totally unaware of this side of our culture till about a year ago. We tried to tell them, but the problem with the Americans is they think that anyone who talks and walks like them is a good guy and that they can work with them. But if people look different and dress differently, or if their religious or cultural principles are alien to them, they must be a bad guy and so should be avoided.

"So the MIT professor is a good guy, even if he has no role in Iraq; and the old man in fancy dress and with a straggly beard will be ignored, even though he is an Iraqi. There's an underlying prejudice against a culture and behaviour patterns that they don't get and this continues to undermine the American understanding of Iraqi society. This is why they face rising military resistance. They throw Iraqis to the ground at their barricades, they tear off their headdress and they put their boots on the back of their heads not realising that, for an Iraqi, these are reasons enough to want to kill them. The use of sniffer dogs is offensive to all Iraqis, but to the tribesmen it is mortally offensive, especially near women. This is a society in which feuds run for generations and there is a very high honour system. So the Americans will find that many of the attacks on them are about avenging the honour of Iraqis they have killed. When they kill someone's wife or son or brother, the family will seek revenge – it's as simple as that. It's the start of the cycles of violence. You have US servicemen who are scared kids from California and New York who don't have a clue, who are dumped in rural communities under commanders who put them in the line of fire because they also don't have a clue. The average Iraqi doesn't see the Americans reopening a school or a hospital, but they do see their lives being continually disrupted, so they become humiliated and disgruntled. Throw in with that the terrorist activity of the remnants of the Saddam regime and the influx of Islamic groups that the Americans have allowed over our borders and you can see that the US is creating a phenomenal number of enemies who, after thirty-five years of dictatorship, are more than willing to pick up a weapon and vent their frustration on easy targets."

There seems to be a gulf in the appreciation of the power and the political and cultural sensitivities of Iraq's sheikhs between the US military officials who have to deal with the tribes on a daily basis and their ideological bosses in Baghdad and in Washington. In an interview in the *mudhef* of Sheikh Ali Bin Mohammed al-Menshed on the edge of the Samawa Desert, near Nassiriya, Lieutenant Colonel John J. Bryant initially defended the US effort to reconstruct Iraq. After a pause, however, he conceded, "In terms of the resources we have, the challenge is huge. My budget is thousands of dollars, not millions; and we have soldiers using the money from their own pockets to get equipment for the village communities." He was speaking during the first months of the occupation and the issue that challenged him most was the tribes and their culture: "It's a huge eye-opener. My men worked previously in South and Central America, so it's been quite difficult to understand things here." The power of the sheikhs was, he acknowledged, "awesome". "We just don't understand it. At a meeting with a couple of sheikhs and a lot of citizens, we were talking about how our colleagues in other parts of Iraq were having more problems than we did. What the citizens said was, 'If the sheikhs want us to be kind to the Americans, then we will be kind.' In a nutshell, that told me a whole lot! There is a financial part to every deal, and if an aid group or the US comes into an area, then the sheikh needs to be seen as having brought them in."

Further north in Falluja, a youthful lieutenant colonel, Chris Hickey, the senior coalition commander in the region, was upfront about his ignorance: "The hardest thing for me coming into the region is to understand the local power relations. I've got seven tribes here, but I'm still learning where they are and who's in charge. It's very confusing. I've been here for a few weeks, and I ask the mayor for a meeting with the sheikhs, but later I'm told that the people he lined up for me are not the real sheikhs!" Almost in desperation he asked me, "What does a sheikh look like? I go to meetings with people who dress and look like sheikhs, but they don't carry a sheikh ID card. So till I figure this out, I have to stand above tribal politics and deal with the higher goals of safety, peace and prosperity. We know what's wrong with this town, but it can't be fixed properly till organisations like the United Nations come in. But those people will not come here till we have a safe and secure environment.

My point of leverage with the sheikhs is if they want to achieve these goals, they will have to make this a secure place. Eleven attacks on my vehicles and convoys in the last week is not my idea of 'secure'. I've read my *Lawrence of Arabia*. But I was trained to deploy a squadron on a battle-field with choppers, Bradleys and artillery. Instead I'm going to meetings of the city council and trying to keep local roads safe."

In Falluja, Hickey's predecessors had tentatively embraced tribal values. They started to pay "blood money" to injured Iraqis and to the families of those killed by US forces after the local mayor had argued that without such payments they would be locked into a cycle of escalating violence. Hickey explained, "It's $1500 for a death and up to $500 for injuries, provided the victims were not involved in shooting at us when they are hit. We're keeping up the payments in the hope that five generations of Iraqis will not come after us for revenge killings. The idea was to bring down the level of violence – and it works to a degree." Speaking before the explosive April 2004 crisis at Falluja, he told me, "There has been a fall-off in the revenge attacks, but those who are simply opposed to us are still shooting at us. It's hard to impose Western ideas of democracy instantly, so we're taking baby steps first. The mayor of Falluja was select-ed by the sheikhs. Is that democracy? Not as we know it, but it's a major step for Iraqis and we just have to do things incrementally. This is much more difficult than Operation Desert Storm. That was a conventional war in the desert. It was fast and the only dealing I had with Iraqis was when we took them prisoner. This is more complex. I have to understand a social and political system and deal with endless small-scale threats instead of a conventional military force."

Inside the hyper-protected bunker of the Coalition Provisional Authority in central Baghdad, there was an early expectation that Iraqis would outgrow their tribal ways just as soon as they came to understand the gift of Western democracy. Likening tribal Iraqis to the farm labour-ers who flocked to British cities during the industrial revolution, a senior official, who asked not to be named, said, "It will be interesting to see how it plays out, because the Baath Party tried to leapfrog Iraq from the 1600s to the twentieth century, and it didn't do a very good job. The significance of the bigger tribes doesn't escape me. But if it was as easy as talking to five or six sheikhs to put a stop to the violence, we'd have done it. We're not that dense." He insisted that the tribes were not a significant issue for Washington, claiming that they would have a role if they co-operated and saw things in the same light as the US: "If it is a question of harnessing the power of the tribes, then it's a question of finding tribal leaders who can operate in a post-tribal environment. We'll have to rely on these people to carry the message of what the new democracy is about." But another senior adviser to Paul Bremer, also reluctant to be named, marvelled at how the sheikhs have emerged – still powerful – from the obscurity of what he described as "the government over-burden of the last forty-five years". He seemed to have a better grasp of the Iraqi reality: "I'm surprised by how resilient the tribal structure has been in surviving the wear and tear of all those years. Socially, you'd think that Saddam would have left Iraq in the same shambles that he left it economically. But the tribal culture seems to have had more staying power than the Baath Party philosophy."

That was in the northern summer of 2003. Since then there have been occasional signs the US and its coalition partners are slowly moving towards a better understanding of the tribes and their power. Courted in the right way by an enlightened US officer, sheikhs provided the information that led to the arrest of half a dozen of the Americans' most-wanted Iraqis; and in the north, a 230-strong Sheikh Force has been set up jointly by the US and a UK security firm to protect a local ammunition dump and oil pipelines.

In central Iraq in January 2004, my colleague Larry Kaplow, of the *Atlanta Journal Constitution*, witnessed a remarkable arrest effort by US Capt Karl Pfuetze who claimed that as "the US was the biggest tribe on the block", he had resorted to his version of tribal tactics to make arrests. This involved shouting threats, through a translator, that he would "destroy the whole tribe ... put fifty people of the Jassat tribe in jail every day until they freakin' turn 'em in." Pfuetze had fingered Jassat tribesmen as the culprits in a killing spree in which two US and eighteen Iraqi truckers and security guards had died.

These latter tactics seemed a long way removed from the new "reconciliation strategy" adopted by the US early in 2004, a tentative response to a damning Pentagon report that had blamed America's failure to understand the tribes for alienating thousands of potential supporters. The report, a copy of which was leaked to *The Boston Globe*, said that the US's "lack of inclusion of tribal leaders in policy-making and implementation shames tribal leaders and ignores thousands of years of Arab socio-political culture ... we are engaged in a game without a clear appreciation of the rules and rituals that regulate play." The work of a three-man military team in Baghdad, it said with an enlightenment that seems to have been ignored: "Counter-insurgency efforts must focus on returning honour to the Iraqi people, engaging tribal decision makers, and work within cultural norms to build a modern democratic Iraqi nation. The greatest wildcard that the insurgents can exploit is the coalition's lack of cultural understanding and ability to communicate with the rural population to reinforce the idea that [US] policies are attacks against cultural norms, honour and way of life."

The remarkable thing about the likes of the late Sheikh Malik al-Kharbit and Sheikh Ali Bin Mohammed al-Menshed is that although their tribes come first, they are – or were – well disposed to Washington and its plans for Iraq. They are on the American side for as long as they can see a place for themselves in those plans. Sheikh Ali's role in assisting America as it plotted Saddam's downfall was as remarkable as was Malik's. It took great courage for the sheikhs of Iraq to ignore Saddam's call to arms against America, but Sheikh Ali went even further, and he did it alone and in secret. He assembled an army of more than 1600 fighters drawn from his own tribe and they fought alongside the Americans against the Iraqi military.

Like the late Malik, Sheikh Ali had his first meeting with the US agents in Jordan almost a year before the March 2003 invasion. It is a story that answers more of the riddle of why Saddam Hussein was pushed over so easily and so quickly.

Sheikh Ali told me that he made his initial approach to the Americans two years earlier through a Saudi Arabian intermediary. It was rebuffed, but several months later a Kuwaiti friend set up a meeting that took place in the deserts of northern Kuwait. "Seven people were at the meeting. I was the only Iraqi and there were three Americans, all in civilian dress." His irritated refusal to say what kind of "civilian" dress they wore suggested that the US agents came disguised as Arabs, but Ali was racing ahead with his story: "The other Iraqi sheikhs were scared to death. I could not tell them what I was doing, but we would meet in secret to discuss the coming war. Saddam's people were watching us all the time, so we'd send messengers to each other's mudhef, to set up meetings in private homes in Nassiriya; or we'd meet for just ten minutes among the guests at a wedding or the mourners at a funeral. In the run-up to the war I spent forty-five days with the Americans. Just before the war we flew into Iraq at night time – eighteen men and five helicopters, each carrying one vehicle. We landed in the desert to safeguard four bridges that were vital crossings on the Euphrates if the Americans were to go north to Baghdad. I was the only Iraqi. It was a decisive hour. All I could think of was getting rid of Saddam. Even before the war started, the Americans had a secret base here at my mudhef. The choppers that flew in the US weapons and equipment landed just over there, but Saddam's men never worked it out. My men moved about in civilian vehicles. First we liberated the west bank of the Euphrates at Nassiriya. I was aware of the enormity of the decision to work with the Americans, but I clutched my heart till it felt like stone and decided to keep it a secret between Allah and myself."

Many of the sheikhs are reticent when it comes to questions about their relationship with the US occupation forces. One local observer insisted that Sheikh Ali seemed to have little to do with the Americans these days because the money they were paying him had dried up; another maintained that he was discreet about his dealings *because* they were still paying him. In defending the Americans, Sheikh Ali said he believed that they did have a "full understanding" of the role of the tribes. That sounded unambiguous enough, until he added pointedly, "But the British have so much more experience in these things. T.E. Lawrence was an intelligent man, and he succeeded in getting into the hearts of our people." The historic role of Lawrence of Arabia is raised again and again by the sheikhs – it is an implicit criticism of the US and its failure to understand the subtleties and sinews of tribal life. The sheikhs separate the performance of Lawrence the man from that of his government, and they take great pride in the fact that in his desire to understand them, the Englishman came close to becoming an Arab. He wore their dress, he ate their food and he lived their life. As we sat on the exotic mats that cover the earthen floor of his goat-hair *mudhef*, Sheikh Ali's pride was overwhelming when I asked if Lawrence came through this part of Iraq. "Oh yes," he said, swelling up. "He sat with my grandfather – where we sit now."

Sheikh Ali wanted to talk about the present, not the past, though. He was desperate for Washington to cut a deal with the sheikhs, just as Saddam had done and the kings before him. "The Americans have made a great mistake in disbanding the old Iraqi army and the police. This is why we have the resistance and the bombings, the killing and the looting," he said. "American soldiers are being killed every day, but it's their own fault." And the earlier warnings I'd been given – that the continuing chaos in today's Iraq was the sheikhs' opening bid for the Americans to cut them in on the action – reverberated when he told me, "We're supposed to be grateful and to thank them for our liberation, but we have this security problem. My first request to the Americans after the war was that they should get the tribe to do security. I was the first sheikh to put this to them but, sadly, they would not listen."

Baghdad remains a city of fear, patrolled by tanks and guns, where kidnappings and murder are rife. There's gunfire through most days and nights, punctuated from time to time by explosions that cause little apparent disruption to the rhythm of the city – unless runners or the internet report that bodies are again piling up in the city's over-used morgues. The Americans have started reducing their street patrols, pulling back to bases. Their place has been taken by an anxious, incompetent and ill-equipped new Iraqi police force and dozens of public security organisations and politically backed militias.

Hundreds of thousands of second-hand cars have been imported since the war, and they add to the city's gridlock, as do snap US checkpoints and road closures that block traffic entirely or reduce peak-hour movement to a single-lane snarl where the pace is set by donkey-carts, wheel-barrows and hand-carts. Petrol queues have shortened since December 2003. A mobile phone system is staggering into life, and some of the telephone exchanges bombed by the Americans during the war are expected to come back into service any time now. There are still power blackouts every day, though, and there is no guarantee about the quality of the drinking water. Raw sewage runs in garbage-strewn streets. Attendance numbers at some mosques – Shiite and Sunni – are down because of random bombings and shootings; and schools that are robbed repeatedly are getting janitors and other staff to double as armed guards. Bandits control much of the highways, using fast-moving BMWs and Thuraya satellite phones to track the motorists they choose to rob, to capture and – in some cases – to murder.

Geert Van Moorter, an activist Belgian doctor who visits Iraq regularly, is generous when he accepts the CPA estimate of Iraqi unemployment of 35 per cent. He comments, "Others say it's more likely between 40 and 60 per cent; but say the CPA is right, that's about one-third of the population whose purchasing power has been reduced since the war. People in work are getting better pay, but there was no rice in this month's food distribution, vegetables and meat have doubled in price, and cooking gas is five to ten times more expensive than under Saddam. In five hospitals I revisited this week, there has been no change in the buildings or medical equipment; they have over-the-counter drugs but they lack many of the specialist drugs they need, especially for chronic patients." In this environment many are desperate. As my driver waited to make a U-turn in the city, a girl of about six leapt into the traffic, crossing three fast-moving lanes to beg at the car window. It was not till we had gone through the turn and started to speed away that we realised the child was still hanging from the side of the car. Later in the day we went through the same intersection and a small boy was there with his hand out. A colleague travelling with us told him, "Maybe later ...", to which he replied in American English, "Fuck you too!"

In the mayhem, Baghdad has been carved into a series of Western security bubbles. There is the Green Zone, Paul Bremer's sprawling riverside bunker, for which the Pentagon is about to let a $US100 million privatised security contract; there is the blast-walled compound of the Palestine and Sheraton hotels, which have their own militia; foreign embassies are grouping and fortifying; and Western business and the foreign media have all but withdrawn behind concrete, wire and guns, venturing out reluctantly and accompanied always by security vehicles fore and aft. Pity the poor Iraqis. They're outside the walls and at the other end of the guns, unprotected from the bombers and criminals who have run amok, robbing and kidnapping in a security vacuum in which it is nigh on impossible for the new Iraqi police force to get traction, squeezed as it is between so much military muscle. Much is made of Iraq's new free press, but the TV market is dominated by the much-maligned al-Jazeera and al-Arabia channels; most of the 200 new newspapers, to which Washington points as proof of a burgeoning democracy in the making, are propaganda sheets that protect the vested interests of one political party or another rather than foster constructive debate. And if the US does not like the tone of their reporting, it shuts them down – a little like Saddam once did.

Many of the new political parties have their own armed militias. Like every key issue confronting the new Iraq, their role has been ducked in the framing of the nation's controversial interim constitution; the Americans have not dared to bite the bullet. So for now the ranks of the Shiite-backed Badr Brigade engage in security and policing in neighbourhoods loyal to their party; the Kurdish *Peshmerga* stand ready to defend their territory in the north; and the Sunni militias are already at war. It could well be that the much predicted civil war has already begun.

The exile-dominated, US-appointed Iraq Governing Council has been a trial for Washington and, ultimately, a failed attempt to predetermine the fate of liberated Iraq. Every issue bogs down in a three-cornered squabble, where invariably the only decision made is the one to fudge the key issue until later. A store of time bombs is thereby being laid up for when the US relinquishes political control of the country. Now, after pillorying the United Nations mercilessly in the run-up to war and with nowhere else to turn, Washington is pleading with UN Secretary-General Kofi Annan to send his teams back, to help the US out of an impasse concerning how Iraq should be governed until the elections scheduled for January 2005. UN teams made brief visits in March–April 2004, but the Secretary-General warned Washington that security would have to improve significantly before the UN would come back to Iraq full-time. The level of tension between the increasingly obstreperous Shiites and the Americans was palpable when I asked a Shiite strategist about the confused decision-making of the US when it came to controlling Iraq's borders. He thought for a while about what seemed a peculiar move to tighten only the border with Iran when the constant cry from Washington is that most foreign fighters are entering Iraq from Syria. Then he snapped, "I don't know what's in the Americans' minds. But you know how they think: they always do the wrong thing in the wrong place at the wrong time."

Beyond motherhood statement, none of the Iraqi players has enunciated a clear view of what the new Iraq might be. The most powerful of them, the enigmatic al-Sistani, chooses his words very carefully. But like Sheikh Ali Hussein al-Nida, the tribal leader I spoke to near Saddam's home village, al-Sistani has taken to reminding the Iraqi tribes of their role in the 1920s challenge to British occupation, telling them in a newspaper advertisement, "We want you to be the revolutionaries. You should have as big a role today as you had in the revolution of 1920." And Ayatollah Ali al-Hakim al-Safi, a senior cleric in Basra who counselled Shiites at a January demonstration to be restrained, warned at the same time, "If we find peaceful means are no longer available to us, we will have to seek other methods."

Most US casualties happen in the so-called Sunni Triangle, north and west of Baghdad. Appalling and all as this death and maiming is, American voters initially seemed to see it as an acceptable price to pay for mopping up what they were told were the remnants of Saddam's regime. But early in 2004 the resistance – aided by foreign forces assumed by the US and others to include al-Qaeda, but about whom little is known – took the fight out of the Sunni Triangle and into the heart of the Shiite and Kurdish communities in a calculated attempt to bring on the civil war.

With no regard for the rebel norms of keeping the population on side, the Iraqi insurgency has been brutally effective. It repeatedly penetrates the tightest US security. In November 2003, insurgents used donkey-drawn carts to get missiles within striking range of three of the city's most heavily guarded buildings; they have thumbed their noses at the US several times, striking deep behind the blast walls of the highly protected US Green Zone in the heart of Baghdad, and mauling the Al-Rasheed Hotel with missile and mortar barrages. In mid-May 2004, they mounted a suicide-bomb attack on an Iraqi Governing Council convoy as it entered the main US compound, killing the serving president of the IGC, Ezzedine Salim, and eight others. Nothing could have illustrated more dramatically how fragile was the US grip on Iraq. The insurgents have also succeeded in drawing the US into provocative, Israeli-inspired tactics of collective punishment: villages ringed with razor wire; homes and factories demolished; the detention of suspects' families to force them to surrender. In December 2003 the Coalition Provisional Authority boasted that in one 24-hour period it had raided 1620 suspects to net 107 arrests. The Americans were pleased with themselves, but do the maths – 107 arrests left more than 1500 angry Iraqis at large to bad-mouth the "liberating" US forces.

Early in 2004, attacks on American forces fell to about half of their peak numbers four months earlier, and the Americans began a troop rotation in preparation for the 30 June hand-over, replacing 100,000-plus troops with fresh new kids from Texas and Idaho who had little or no combat experience and no experience of Iraq. Midway through the rotation, all hell broke loose. In April, the world watched in horror as a Sunni street mob in the restive town of Falluja hacked to pieces the bodies of four American security contractors after incinerating the vehicles in which they entered the town. In the same week, seeming not to appreciate the likely consequences, the Americans decided to turn up the heat under Moqutada al-Sadr. In a flash, the occupation forces of George W. Bush were fighting on two fronts – against a Shiite uprising in support of al-Sadr across the south of the country; and against a ferocious tribes-backed defence of Falluja when the Americans besieged the town of 300,000 people and then went in, guns blazing. Their oft-repeated claim to be in control of Iraq went out the window with a request by the generals to Washington – granted immediately – for another 20,000 troops for Iraq, the country in which Washington had predicted they would be welcomed with flowers and music.

When Iraqis write this chapter of their history, they will debate whether the siege of Falluja or the international scandal which erupted only weeks later over the US treatment of prisoners at Abu Ghraib was the critical turning point in the conflict. Falluja's refusal to buckle in the face of

American power is now celebrated in Iraqi songs, and newspapers in the region publish poetry on the stout-heartedness of the city's people. The attack on the security contractors was grotesque but effective. It shot down the Washington-inspired myth that no ordinary or decent Iraqi would have anything to do with the resistance and simultaneously lured the US into a badly thought-out military response which produced a death toll so shocking that when the Americans called on Iraqi politicians to stand with them against the "two-bit thugs" of Falluja, they were met with silence. And, after all that firepower had been unleashed, the first demand the Americans dropped was the one they had used to justify the siege – that the townspeople must be made to hand over the killers of the four Americans. Looked at through Iraqi eyes, virtually every aspect of the Falluja crisis represented a defeat for the Americans. And after Falluja came Abu Ghraib, a self-inflicted US wound that will reverberate for years in Iraq and across the region, casting the Americans in Iraqi and Arab eyes as not so different from Saddam Hussein.

Having assumed control of Iraq, probably the only option now open to George W. Bush is to tough it out. US strategic interests require a long-term military presence in Iraq, and the prospect of civil war demands that Washington maintain or increase its numbers in the country. But domestic politics in the US requires signs of progress, so in desperation Washington points to the relative peace of the north and the south as a substantial achievement. While the centre of Iraq, especially Baghdad, remains a cauldron, however, it is virtually impossible to create the half-normal living conditions that might inspire in Iraqis some hope for the future. Anger simmers at the prospect of a long wait for adequate and reasonably priced supplies of electricity, petrol and cooking gas. If the US stays the course with its timetable for a fully elected new Iraqi govern-ment – as Bush insists that it will – it's still likely to be many years before it can be demonstrated that Iraqis are in control of Iraq. Delays on both fronts create a perfect environment for guerrilla war, during and beyond which hopes for democracy in Iraq will simply wither.

Ayatollah al-Sistani and the tribal sheikhs have become the pivot points in this unique American exercise in fixing broken nations. Apart from West Germany and Japan, only two of the sixteen US-led efforts in nation rebuilding in the last century – namely, tiny Panama and Grenada – continued to function as democracies ten years after US intervention. It's still early days in Afghanistan, but much of the country remains under the boot of autocratic warlords. None of the other candidates for a Washington make-over in the last 100 years was an Islamic nation. At best, the Arab countries embraced by the US might be described as "liberalised autocracies" – Egypt, Jordan, Morocco, Algeria and Kuwait. They have constitutions in flowery language that purport to guarantee many of the rights we take for granted in Western democracies, but their leaders survive by control and repression – their self-serving security apparatuses are ugly and their parliamentary oppositions a joke. In truth, excepting Israel, democracy does not exist in the Middle East, and this despite the sorrow of so much Western intervention in the region over the years. Can it be planted in Iraq, which has known only occupation and puppet statehood, repression and ruthlessness since it was set up by Britain in the 1920s?

Supporters of the White House drive for democracy claim it is racist heresy to even pose this question, but for many other observers the reality of the Middle East means that any attempt to foist the bottom-up principles and rights of democracy onto societies that are so top-down driven will require a decades-long commitment, if not longer. Or, more likely, the attempt will simply fail. Few of what the experts call the pre-conditions for democracy exist. Compared with the historical backdrop of post-war Japan and Germany, Iraq's history of colonialism, imposed monarchy, fascist revolution, Arab nationalism and Islam leaves little or no room for tolerance and trust. In this patriarchal society, much is made of the lack of rights for women, but in the Iraqi culture nearly all surrender many of their rights – what we in the West see as their democratic rights – either to their tribe or their religion. The tribal sheikhs are born to rule and many of the imams exercise the same hereditary powers, taking authority from a direct ancestral link to Mohammed the Prophet or by imposing a strict Koranic code on their congregations.

That blood carries power in Iraq just as it carries oxygen was borne out when I arrived for an appointment at the home of Sayed Kamal Adine al-Mukudas al-Kurfi, one of al-Sistani's deputies in Baghdad. It was the sayed's son, Ahmad, who sat behind his father's desk in a book-lined study and announced that because his father was indisposed, he would take the interview, as though this was the most natural thing in the world. Unless the Iraqi constitution was written by an elected body, it would be an empty vessel – "illegitimate", he said. And in the face of US attempts to provide checks and balances in the constitution to mark the divisions in the nation, he added, "A small part of society cannot be allowed to contradict the wishes of the majority." He warmed to what he saw as American attempts at manipulation: "The US is trying to shape Iraq by using local political parties who think the US will keep them in power, but it will not succeed." And then, just a little disingenuously: "We don't care if it is a Shiite government. [But] we have 65 per cent of the people, so let the election decide. There is talk of civil war that does not worry these other parties. But the Shiites will not let that happen. They have attacked us already, but we will continue to debate them … but most Shiites have been in the military and, if we have to, we can fight with weapons. This is the first time in our history that the Shiites might run the country."

In a policy paper on democracy in Iraq for the conservative, Washington-based Cato Institute, Patrick Basham ruminates, "In such an environment, most people adopt a political passivity that acts as a break on the development of the principles – such as personal responsibility and self-help – central to the development of economic and political liberalism. Hence, political freedom is an alien concept to most Iraqis." And the educated middle class that might have provided the fertile ground in which to plant democracy in Iraq all but fled the country during Saddam's rule. Basham laments, "The remnants can contribute to the democratisation of their country, but the current middle class does not constitute a critical mass capable of moderating and channelling political debate in a secular, liberal fashion."

Out of this feuding, vengeful mess, the Americans must do the near impossible – craft a leadership structure which, like it or not, will be Shiite-dominated but which is acceptable to all; one that does not sanction revenge against the Sunnis, who have demonstrated that they are ready to fight; and which can tolerate and nurture Iraq's other terrified minorities and stop them turning on each other, as they already have done – Kurds, Turkomen and Christians. More than a year of US occupation has done nothing to resolve these tensions. The US intervention in Iraq – for reasons now utterly discredited – has unleashed an ethnic and religious maelstrom that draws on disparate Iraqi forces. The Sunnis can fight brutally, but they are unlikely to reassert their Baathist supremacy; they can frustrate the Shiite hunger for dominance, but in doing so they might well drag them into a bloody war; and the Kurds are so confident of their position, as much because of their own bravura as because of the debt of protection that America owes them, that they risk inviting attacks by both Shiites and Sunnis. The prospect is that Iraq will become Beirut writ large. All three factions have their arms and their turf – Kurds in the north, Sunnis in the centre and Shiites in the south. Some tribes are both Shiite and Sunni, and in the middle of the country sits Baghdad, a volatile mix of all three, which in the event of civil war would be the site of a bloody free-for-all.

All are trapped in a perceptual twilight zone where the fundamentals cannot be aligned. The Americans harp on about the collapse of Saddam Hussein and tell Iraqis how lucky they are to be free. Looking at the prospect of tens of thousands of foreign troops on their soil for years to come, Iraqis say "No. We are occupied." The chances are, the violence that has been mounting since April 2003 is a mere rumble compared to what is in store. The trouble is, we won't know until it's too late. Traditionally

Iraqis will tell you what you want to hear, while at the same time manoeuvring towards their own objective. As the country exploded during the Shiite uprising against the US occupation in April 2004, I wondered aloud to my translator Salaam if the Americans knew to whom they were talking. I was left with a sense that two dialogues were taking place in Iraq – one between the US and Iraq in which the Iraqis told the Americans what they wanted to hear; and a second, more powerful discourse among Iraqis themselves as they set the scene for a post-30 June carve-up of the country … and probably of each other.

"Exactly!" said Salaam.

Amanda Vanstone

Robert Manne's essay *Sending Them Home: Refugees and the New Politics of Indifference* is the latest addition to a genre that is popular within a small but articulate section of the Australian community. Dear to the heart of this collection of church leaders, journalists and academics is the view that a large section of the Australian community is racist and xenophobic. Perhaps because they feel unappreciated by the wider Australian community, many Australian intellectuals have tended to regard their "ordinary" brothers and sisters as redneck and racist. The views of this bunch in relation to asylum seeking are built on a psychological foundation of denial about some very uncomfortable realities.

The first is that global inequality and the growth of people smuggling combine to undermine the integrity of the international system, designed to grant protection to those people most in need.

The reality is that 1.2 billion people live in absolute, dire poverty, surviving on less than a US$1 a day. The world has millions of vulnerable people and people smugglers will always prey on that vulnerability.

Secondly, our tender-minded intellectuals cannot face the fact Australia's capacity to provide places for refugees is necessarily finite. If we accept as a refugee someone whose claims are doubtful, we do so at the expense of someone else whose claims for permanent protection may be stronger. We can only help so many people and nothing can change that.

Focused on his own compassion and always ready to point an accusing finger, Robert Manne seems impervious to these uncomfortable realities. If he had taken a long hard look at some basic facts, he might have been much slower to condemn governments tasked with making the tough decisions these facts impose.

According to the International Organisation for Migration there are an estimated 30 to 40 million illegal immigrants worldwide. Annually, around 500,000 illegal migrants enter Europe and another 700,000 enter the USA. It is obvious to anyone with an open mind that the overwhelming majority of these people are not refugees.

Most of the 10 million people the United Nations estimates are genuine refugees live in camps where life is hard, generally much harder than in many of the source countries for Australia's recent unlawful entrants. They are not wandering the world looking for a place to stop. Of course it is true that genuine refugees still cross borders to seek protection in Western countries. And it is important that access to a refugee determination process and a place of protection be available to all who need to seek protection.

Robert Manne is not moved by the plight of people in camps, however; they, it seems, are the world's problem, not Australia's.

But the reality today, which is confirmed by the statistics of asylum claims in Western countries, is that the overwhelming majority of claimants in recent years have not been found to be refugees.

In the Netherlands, for example, in 2002 only 0.6 per cent of claimants were given refugee status and a total of 12.2 per cent were given some form of protection. In Germany less than 10 per cent of claimants were successful in 2002 in gaining any form of protection.

In many cases, the people who arrive illegally in Western countries have travelled through countries where they could have found protection. Indeed, many of them may have enjoyed long-term protection in another country. Their motives for proceeding to the wealthy West are obvious. They want a better standard of living. This is no doubt a fact that causes discomfort for the guilt merchants.

Robert Manne admits that "very large numbers" of people have sought to exploit refugee laws by "claims of persecution which are either exaggerated or invented". However, he does not dwell on this point or face the scale of the problem. The psychology of denial requires him to move on quickly.

With hundreds of thousands of people flowing into affluent European Western countries and most claims for asylum being rejected, there is inevitably a build-up of people without legal status. The many legal obstacles to removal of unsuccessful claimants in most jurisdictions are a major part of the problem.

In Europe, in particular, there have been relatively few removals. European countries have emphasised the importance of voluntary return. If failed asylum seekers are not removed, then assessment processes seem pointless and they can be allowed to move slowly.

What has happened, to be candid about it, is that the Europeans have made a virtue out of necessity. They cannot easily prevent arrivals, nor easily remove people, so they have been happy for their response to be portrayed as an exercise in compassion. Things are changing, however. The Europeans are more actively tackling these issues. Some of the approaches being considered mirror those taken by the Australian government. Robert Manne needs to open his eyes and see what is happening.

The Netherlands, a longstanding champion of the UN Refugee Convention, has recently confronted the problem of failed asylum seekers. In February this year the Dutch Parliament legislated to introduce involuntary removal for failed asylum seekers. This applies to an estimated 26,000 people who have arrived since the introduction of new asylum legislation in 2001. Some still have avenues of appeal open, but they now know that involuntary removal stands at the end of the process.

The sad reality is that the international system of protection for people fleeing persecution is under threat from economically motivated illegal migration. Unless the integrity of the asylum system can be ensured – and this means that failed asylum seekers must be returned – the whole system is in danger of falling into disrepute. Attacks on the return of failed asylum seekers are undermining the integrity of the 1951 Convention.

Unless governments around the world actively discourage the use of people smugglers the United Nation's system becomes a second-class system, available only to those who cannot afford to pay a people smuggler.

The hope of an orderly system of resettlement for those refugees most in need of a new home is under threat from those who are happy for people smugglers to decide who gets resettled

Robert Manne makes much of the fact a large percentage of boat people in the years leading up to *Tampa* had been successful in their asylum claims in Australia. Yet he does not acknowledge that this suggests that Australia's system is fair and that people whose claims are not recognised should leave Australia. His world is a world where everyone can have what they want, where no one gains something else at the expense of anyone else. This is the attitude of the armchair commentator, not someone with actual responsibility for making the tough decisions of government.

Manne rejects any connection between places granted "onshore", that is, asylum claims approved for people who have arrived in Australia one way or another, and "offshore places", that is, places granted to people outside Australia. He cannot face the reality that having set the number of places to be taken by refugees, any place taken by an "onshore" grantee will be at the expense of an "offshore" applicant.

Yet this is the way our system works. We grant as many places per year as we think we reasonably can. In 2004–05 it will increase from 12,000 to 13,000. If any of these places are unfilled in the year in which they are allocated, they are added to the allocation of the following year. Our commitment to providing protection to people most in need is clear and transparent. Where a person on a temporary protection visa no longer needs protection and leaves Australia, the place vacated will be added to the allocation available for that year. This is a transparent process. It makes brutally clear the fact that we live in a world where all of the good things we take for granted in Australia are very limited, globally.

Nowhere is Robert Manne's state of denial more evident than in relation to the Pacific Solution. The decision to hear asylum seekers' claims outside Australia has been very effective in stemming the flow of asylum seekers into Australia by boat.

The success of the Pacific Solution is something that seems to have Robert Manne shifting uncomfortably in his armchair. The objective of asylum seekers heading for Australia is to get a foothold in Australia, rather than to gain protection that may well be available elsewhere. If they make it to Australia, Australian courts and Australian refugee advocates offer a hope that people can stay, irrespective of the strength of any refugee claim. For claimants in detention, the advocates fight for release. For people granted a temporary visa, the advocates campaign for permanent visas.

Manne cites the case of the *Minasa Bone*, the Indonesian fishing vessel carrying fourteen Turkish Kurds that landed on Melville Island in 2003. He notes that the excision of Melville Island from Australia's migration zone effectively prevented claims from being made in Australia. He fails, however, to mention how this story ends, with offshore processing. When the fourteen were given the opportunity to have their claims heard in Indonesia by the United Nations High Commission for Refugees (UNHCR), seven did not even bother to take this opportunity – they caught the first plane back to Turkey. The rest had their claims refused and left shortly after that. In interviews with the media before leaving, they described their motives as a desire to set up kebab shops and earn $8000 a week, and to meet Australian women.

Robert Manne and other refugee advocates never explain why they are unwilling to abide by the umpire's rules. It is evident, however, that they are sympathetic to any claim made by an asylum seeker and ready to reject as biased the assessments made by Immigration Department officials or the Refugee Review Tribunal.

Part of Robert Manne's problem is his unwillingness to consider numbers.

He wants us to focus on the 12,000 people who sought to reach Australia in the period in question. "There is little we can do for the overwhelming majority of the fourteen million." He calls this "the ethics of proximity". I call it the ethics of tokenism. This is just the salving of a conscience that cannot face the ugly reality of millions of refugees, let alone the much bigger moral problem of global inequality.

The most moral and compassionate way of responding to this horrendous problem is not to take the easy way out by accepting only those on your doorstep, but to determinedly take first those most in need. Largely they will not be people who can afford to pay people smugglers.

The fact is that Australia's refugee and humanitarian program, which will have 13,000 places in 2004–05, can play an important part in helping the UNHCR to work with affected governments to solve the problems of refugees in camps. The UNHCR's preference is always for people to return to their homes if this is at all possible. Where this is not possible, resettlement can play a critical role in resolving longstanding problems.

Over the past decade Australia has welcomed a million migrants from all over the world. Included in this are more than a hundred thousand refugee and humanitarian entrants. This is not a sign of a country that is xenophobic or racist. It is not cold or lacking in compassion. But clearly the majority of Australians, who support the government's policy, are able to face harsh realities that leave tender-minded intellectuals in denial.

Robert Manne and other woolly-minded critics of our refugee policy need to face the fact that their armchair moralising is not some harmless excess of compassion. It provides critical support to the burgeoning people-smuggling business, which in turn threatens the future of the international refugee protection system. If this thought does not get through the net of denial that lets him sleep peacefully every night, he could reflect on the responsibility he would hold for any future loss of life through people getting into leaky boats and attempting to enter Australia unlawfully.

Amanda Vanstone

Robert Manne

Although I am grateful that Senator Amanda Vanstone has responded to *Sending Them Home*, it is difficult to believe either that she has read the essay attentively or given much thought to her reply. Senator Vanstone begins by including me among a "small but articulate section of the Australian community" who, she claims, believe their fellow Australians to be "racist and xenophobic". In fact in *Sending Them Home* there is no discussion which might lead readers to think I hold such a view. In the essay I use the word "racist" only once and then in a context entirely unconnected to the opinions of the Australian people. The word "xenophobic" never appears. Whenever I am asked, in public discussions, whether I think the Australian people or indeed the ministers in the Howard government are racists, I reply that I do not. While both the Australian people and their government might be blind to the suffering inflicted here on Middle Eastern Islamic refugees – in a way that would not be tolerated with regard, for example, to white Zimbabwean refugees – this blindness is, in my opinion, different to racism according to the generally accepted meaning of that word.

Having mischaracterised my view of the Australian people, Senator Vanstone reminds me that "1.2 billion people live in absolute, dire poverty, surviving on less than a US $1 a day" and that "the world has millions of vulnerable people and people smugglers will always play on that vulnerability." How these vulnerable people, living on $1 a day, can afford to buy a passage from a people smuggler is not explained.

Senator Vanstone continues with a discussion of doubtful relevance concerning the vast number of "illegal immigrants who enter Europe and North America" each year. Helpfully she points out that "it is obvious to anyone with an open mind that the overwhelming majority of these people are not refugees." Obviously, I do not disagree. Indeed, as elsewhere Senator Vanstone acknowledges, in *Sending Them Home* I argue that, "In Europe and North America very large numbers of people from both the non-Western and post-Communist worlds have sought residence in the West through the exploitation of existing refugee law, that is by claims of persecution which are either exaggerated or invented." The point of this argument was that, quite unlike the experience of Europe and North America, more than 90 per cent of the "fourth-wave" asylum seekers who reached Australia by boat between 1999 and 2001 were found by the rigorous Australian refugee determination process to be bona fide refugees. That this was so points to what is called in *Sending Them Home* "the fundamental paradox" of Australia's treatment of asylum seekers who arrive without valid visas, namely "the discrepancy between the smallness of the size of the asylum seeker 'problem' and the height of the anti-asylum seeker wall". It is obvious that no Western country has treated asylum seekers as cruelly as Australia has done in recent years — with our unique combination of unreviewable mandatory detention, temporary protection visas for proven refugees, military repulsion and offshore processing detention camps. Why we have treated unauthorised asylum seeker arrivals with unparalleled harshness is a central question of *Sending Them Home*, one which the Minister prefers not to discuss.

Acknowledging that more than 90 per cent of the unauthorised boat arrivals were eventually found to be genuine refugees, Senator Vanstone wonders why I still complain about the continued imprisonment and threatened repatriation of the small number of asylum seekers from Iraq, Afghanistan and Iran who the system eventually decided were not Convention refugees. This is a fair question which demands a serious reply.

As a matter of fact I am not opposed to the forced repatriation of illegal immigrants or of "failed" asylum seekers coming from countries where no threat to their freedom or their safety will arise as a consequence of their involuntary return. I do not, for example, think the Australian government was wrong to repatriate most of the "boat people" from China who arrived in the mid-1990s. I am, however, resolutely opposed to the return of even failed asylum seekers to ferocious police states like theocratic Iran or to the desperately insecure situations of present-day Iraq or Afghanistan. In cases such as these a balance must be struck between the damage to the Australian refugee determination system by an act of mercy to those few hundred asylum seekers whose cases, for one reason or another, have failed, and the damage that might be done either by imprisoning such people for an indefinite time (allowing them slowly to go mad) or sending them home to countries where their lives might be placed seriously at risk. There were only a comparatively small number of asylum seeker arrivals in Australia before October 2001. Since *Tampa* there have been virtually no unauthorised asylum seeker arrivals at all. No real harm will be done to the refugee determination system if Australia now errs on the side of generosity. Very considerable harm will be done to innocent individuals in the case of indefinite imprisonment or forcible return to Iraq, Afghanistan or Iran.

Senator Vanstone claims that I "reject" one element of the government's system for managing its humanitarian migration program – namely the reduction of one "offshore" humanitarian place for every "onshore" asylum seeker claim that succeeds. It is not so much the system that I reject, a system, by the way, not used by some other countries, like the United States, which operate both "onshore" and "offshore" refugee programs. What I reject is the nonsensical, moralistic claims made by ministers of the Howard government that the "onshore" arrivals knowingly "steal places" from the "offshore" refugees living in Third World camps. The idea of theft involves a notion of intention. No asylum seeker reaching Australia could possibly be aware that if their applications for asylum succeed, an offshore applicant will, as a consequence, lose a potential place.

According to Senator Vanstone I am unconcerned about the plight of these refugees in Third World camps. This is not so. She arrives at this false conclusion simply because of my willingness to point to a self-evident truth, namely that since there are perhaps 14 million refugees in the contemporary world, even with the best will in the world, Australia (with an annual quota of 13,000 humanitarian migration places, of which 6000 go to UNHCR refugees) will never be able to offer homes to more than a minuscule fraction of these refugees.

Notwithstanding Senator Vanstone's debating bluster, there is in what she says a genuine problem which needs to be confronted, namely why Australia should provide homes for refugees with the means to make it to our shore while there are so many refugees languishing in Third World camps. One answer is legal. If an asylum seeker arrives on Australian territory seeking refuge, we are obliged, under the UN Refugee Convention we have signed, to assess the validity of the claim. The more important answer, argued at length in Sending Them Home, is moral. In my opinion certain obligations arise from the human relationship established by a call for help made in our presence. I call this "the ethics of proximity". There seems no point in repeating the argument here. Even if Senator Vanstone does not agree with the argument, or understand it, it makes little sense to dismiss it as the "ethics of tokenism", whatever that might mean.

Senator Vanstone claims that I find it embarrassing to acknowledge the "success" of the Howard government policy in driving away asylum seekers by the use of military force. She could not be more wrong. There is a certain kind of liberal sentimentalism which finds it awkward to acknowledge that brutal policies often achieve their ends. I do not think like this. To make an admittedly extreme comparison, just as the Chinese government has very effectively silenced democratic dissent for a decade and a half by the use of tanks at Tiananmen Square, so has the Howard government effectively stemmed the flow of asylum seeker boats by the use of the Australian Navy to drive these potential refugees away. Far from being embarrassed about acknowledging the government's post-*Tampa* success, since mid-2002 (by which time the "achievement" was plain) I have consistently argued that as Australia was now effectively an asylum seeker-free zone, the continued incarceration of "failed" asylum seekers in remote or desert prisons and the continued torment of refugees through the system of temporary protection visas – both parts of an earlier, unsuccessful deterrent strategy – could only be explained as a policy of bureaucratic inertia or as cruelty of an entirely purposeless kind.

The most depressing dimension of Senator Vanstone's reply lies not so much in what she argues but in what she fails to discuss. *Sending Them Home* gives great detail about the shocking consequences for vulnerable asylum seekers of Australia's brutish behaviour, in particular through the stories it tells of Shayan Badraie (mandatory detention), Ahmed Alzilimi and Sondos Ismael (temporary protection) and of the collective experience of the inmates of the quasi-penal colony on Nauru (the Pacific Solution). Senator Vanstone does not deny that her government has inflicted such cruelties on thousands of innocent human beings. Rather she seems to regard this analysis of such little consequence that concerning it she says not one word. In this silence Senator Amanda Vanstone's response provides unwitting confirmation of the central thesis of *Sending Them Home*, of the arrival in Australia of what is called a new politics of indifference.

I would like to believe that this indifference is actually, in the case of this Minister, at least partly feigned. Since the publication of *Sending Them Home* some 130 Afghan asylum seekers on Nauru have been granted refugee status by Australia and been offered homes. Since its publication, mainly for political reasons, several long-term detainees in Australia, including some children, have at long last been released, albeit on bridging visas which ensure that even severely sick women and children have no access to pharmaceutical benefits or Medicare. Finally, as I write, although details have not yet been announced and a Cabinet decision has not yet been made, the press is reporting that the Minister plans a wide-ranging reform of the temporary protection visa system. On balance it now looks a little less likely than it did at the time of writing that the more than 9000 Iraqi, Afghan and Iranian refugees on temporary visas will eventually be repatriated. One can only pray that this is indeed the case.

This response to Senator Vanstone allows me to correct two small errors which appeared in *Sending Them Home*. The Afghan man who died in his bed on Nauru (p. 49) died one year earlier than was claimed. Not all the Afghan hunger strikers last Christmas were Hazaras (p. 56).

Robert Manne
26 May 2004

Carmen Lawrence

As I write, the contemplation of the politics of "indifference" is particularly pungent. It's a week in which we've seen photographs of US soldiers grinning as they sexually humiliate and torture Iraqi prisoners, the US President being more discomfited by the fact that he wasn't told about the allegations than by the offences themselves, and his Defence Secretary "more peeved than sorry" about the affront to decency and the violations of human rights these images depict. The rest of us are shocked out of our complacency, our indifference – at least for the moment – by the power of the images.

As Susan Sontag observes in her recent essay *Regarding the Pain of Others*, "photographs are a means of making 'real' (or 'more real') matters that the privileged and the merely safe might prefer to ignore." The fact that it takes such photographs to disturb our comfort suggests that "our failure is one of the imagination, of empathy; we have failed to hold this reality in mind"; the reality of war – the killing power of modern armies and despots, indiscriminately raining bombs and chemicals on civilians.

How many pictures of death and bloody destruction are we not being shown? And why do these images, above others, command our attention? As one commentator raged, "What is it about these images of sexual humiliation that is more distressing to us than bodies smashed by the bombs in Falluja or children being ripped apart by cluster bombs?"

We have been protected from the images of death that the viewers of al-Jazeera have seen on their screens with relentless frequency – smashed bodies and ruined neighbourhoods. These images will tell them little that they were not already primed to accept. Our delicate sensibilities have been protected from the full force of the invasion of Iraq. Nor, it is true, did we know – or if we knew, much care – about the sadistic brutality of Saddam Hussein. But that cannot exonerate us from understanding what we now see. The fact that Saddam's victims were unremarked and unmourned in the West does not excuse us from responding now.

Sontag observes that such images can give rise to a variety of responses – calls for peace; for revenge. "As objects of contemplation, images of the atrocious can answer several different needs. To steel oneself against weakness. To make oneself more numb. To acknowledge the existence of the incorrigible."

And, she might have added, to mobilise the PR machines. The International Red Cross and human rights groups repeatedly complained about the American military's treatment of Iraqi prisoners. They received very little response from either the military or the US government until the graphic photographs were made public. As Seymour Hersh wrote, "The Army's senior commanders immediately understood they had a problem; a looming political and public-relations disaster that would taint America and damage the war effort."[1]

Manne and Corlett remind us in their excellent essay that indifference is a potent psychological defence against the kindred feelings which might otherwise overwhelm our detachment from the daily toll of killings around the globe, from the suffering of the people who've sought our succour and been penned like animals in the camps on and beyond our shores. If we could see the anguish and suffering of those on Nauru, would we not insist that our government immediately abandon the "Pacific Solution"? Our leaders were careful to prevent us seeing any "humanising" images of those stranded on the *Tampa*, to deny any access – even for lawyers – to those on Nauru, and to prohibit any photographs, videos or media coverage of the conditions in the mainland camps. This suggests that they well understand the power of the image. They appreciate that "indifference" is difficult to sustain when we are confronted with the vivid immediacy of the visual image.

In a speech in 1999, Elie Wiesel, Holocaust survivor and Nobel Peace Prize winner, spoke eloquently of the "the perils of indifference".[2] He surveyed the legacy of the twentieth century, labelling it a "violent century", a century which encompassed two world wars, countless civil wars, a senseless chain of assassinations, civilian bloodbaths in many armed conflicts, the inhumanity in the gulags, the tragedy of Hiroshima and the vile stain of the Holocaust. "So much violence", says Wiesel, and perhaps more surprisingly, "so much indifference".

Indifference, as Wiesel conceives it, is "a strange and unnatural state in which the lines blur between light and darkness, dusk and dawn, crime and punishment, cruelty and compassion, good and evil".

"What are its causes?" he asks, and its "inescapable consequences? Is it a philosophy? Is there a philosophy of indifference conceivable? Can one possibly view indifference as a virtue? Is it necessary at times to practice it simply to keep one's sanity, live normally, enjoy a fine meal and a glass of wine, as the world around us experiences harrowing upheavals?"

"Of course," he says, "indifference can be tempting – more than that, seductive. It is so much easier to look away from victims. It is so much easier to avoid such rude interruptions to our work, our dreams, our hopes." It is, as he points out, "awkward, troublesome, to be involved in another person's pain and despair." Yet there are costs. For the person who is indifferent, "his or her neighbours are of no consequence. And, therefore, their lives are meaningless. Their hidden or even visible anguish is of no interest. Indifference reduces the Other to an abstraction."

Wiesel argues passionately that "to be indifferent to ... suffering is what makes the human being inhuman". In his view, indifference is more dangerous than anger and hatred. He points out that anger can be a stimulus for creativity or for altruism because one is angry at injustice. But, he argues, indifference is never creative. Even hatred may elicit a response. You fight it. You denounce it. You disarm it. Indifference elicits no response. Indifference is not a response.

> Indifference is not a beginning, it is an end. And, therefore, indifference is always the friend of the enemy, for it benefits the aggressor – never his victim, whose pain is magnified when he or she feels forgotten. The political prisoner in his cell, the hungry children, the homeless refugees – not to respond to their plight, not to relieve their solitude by offering them a spark of hope is to exile them from human memory. And in denying their humanity, we betray our own.

It is instructive from this perspective to remember our responses to the terrorist attacks on September 11 – reactions of grief at so many lives cut cruelly short, horror at the unprecedented scale and the cold calculation of the act – all appropriate responses.

Contrast this to the relative indifference shown to the loss of life in Afghanistan which followed. For much of the media, the war in Afghanistan ended with the fall of Kabul, and apart from the search for bin Laden and al-Quaeda, it quickly became yesterday's news although so many civilians are still being killed. As David Edwards points out, a careful reading of the press reports at the time shows that the number of Afghan casualties of the bombing – collateral damage – quickly exceeded the loss of life on September 11.[3] This on top of the decades of civil conflict, brutal repression and starvation. The fate of millions of innocents stranded in refugee camps as a result of the continuing strife in Afghanistan has been a matter of "supreme indifference" in most of the Western media. As Edwards says, "The sheer scale of what has been so casually passed over is extraordinary."

Why universal reactions of condemnation in one case and muted responses or outright indifference in the other? Why such a discrepancy?

Perhaps it's because we can be seduced into believing that we have no obligation to people who do not share our culture or race or religion. Perhaps it's because the differences between "them" and "us" can be magnified to a point where these people become so alien that they tend not to be seen as fully human. They stop existing as beings with whom we share a common humanity. As a consequence, our capacity to empathise with their suffering and take in the nature of the crimes committed against them becomes partially obliterated. So we can feel the full force of the barbaric murders on September 11, but the thousands of civilian casualties in Afghanistan hardly touch us. And we, like the US military, "don't do body counts" in Iraq and blithely catalogue the atrocities committed by Saddam Hussein and his regime while locking up his victims in the desert.

Whatever its parents or its progeny, indifference, as Wiesel reminds us, is the most poisonous of human reactions when action is needed.

Manne and Corlett's essay provides a timely and dispassionate reading of the history of our recent refugee policy, particularly the most recent element of forcible repatriation, and how it both illustrates and is informed by what they call "the new politics of indifference". In seeking to understand why many Australians appear largely indifferent to the fate of asylum seekers, they ask how we could tolerate such a network of "inhumane and destructive quasi-penal institutions" – the Immigration Detention Centres. How could we see the images of children behind the wire and not be moved? How could we accept the Minister's interpretation of "lip sewing" as just another example of "their" calculated attempts to exploit "our" goodness? How could we cheer a Minister of the Crown who refuses to accept that depression is a mental illness and describes a nearly catatonic young boy as "it" – four times in one interview? And how we can stand uncomplaining as the government sends many of them back to the dangerous, life-threatening circumstances from which they fled.

They ask, rhetorically, "Can a political nation lose touch with moral reality?" and conclude that it can and it did when our government refused to allow Ahmed Alzalimi join his grieving wife after the drowning of their three daughters on the SIEV-X; that at that moment, "the cardinal Orwellian political virtue of 'common decency' was nowhere to be found." In like manner, no one in the

Australian government "bothered even to pretend to care about whether the hunger strikers (on Nauru) lived or died".

The ultimate obscenity of the asylum seeker policy is the forcible repatriation of people found to be genuine refugees and those who, for various reasons, cannot return to the countries from which they came. Among the poor souls who face this threat are the Sabian Mandaeans, followers of the teachings of John the Baptist, who have fled from Iran. Together with several hundred other refugees from the repressive regime, these families face forcible deportation as part of the Howard government's secret agreement with the government of Iran. Many have already received notice that they could, at any moment, be sent back. Indeed, several have already been removed without prior warning, and one young man was recently rescued from imminent deportation after an eleventh-hour intervention by sympathetic lawyers. Most of this is happening without any public reaction at all.

The government has persistently refused to make public the contents of the Memorandum of Understanding that details this agreement, telling the Senate and also in answer to one of my questions, that it was "not in the public interest" to make the document public. They have also consistently refused to provide any guarantees for the safety of those deported to Iran, or anywhere else for that matter. This despite the fact that the head of the United Nations Working Group on Arbitrary Detention, Justice Louis Joinet, has made it clear that, having visited Iran to inspect the human rights situation, he came away with deep concerns about the nature of Australia's agreement with Iran, particularly the fact that, "There are no guarantees as to what will happen when they (Australian detainees) are returned to Iran." He also expressed some scepticism about whether so-called voluntary returns would actually be voluntary.

There is no doubt that the Howard government does not regard itself as seriously bound by our international treaty obligations. But even by their degraded standards, this represents a flagrant disregard of the obligations under the Refugee Convention not to return a refugee to "a place where his or her life or liberty is threatened" and of the Torture Convention not to send a person to "a place where there is a real prospect of torture".

While the federal government has insisted that none of the Iranians threatened with forcible deportation are owed protection under Australia's migration laws, many of those facing deportation fear that, in the very act of providing information for their refugee applications, they have exposed themselves to greater danger if they are returned to Iran. This is especially true for those who are easily identified by religion, occupation or region, even if their names are withheld. Louis Joinet told radio journalist Tom Morton that "the very act of fleeing takes on a political complexion" and in certain cases, "this has given rise to persecution." When apprised of this elevated risk to those forced to return, Philip Ruddock stated the implausible conclusion that if Australia's refugee assessment process has found that they are not refugees – i.e. that they do not have a well-founded fear of persecution – then they will not be persecuted. By definition. Yes, Minister.

The Mandaeans, a tiny pre-Christian religious minority, would, almost certainly, be readily identified from Tribunal and Court transcripts. Because their religion is not recognised by the government of Iran, they are subjected to discrimination and denied the normal protections of the law. The Federal Court, in an appeal against a decision of the Refugee Review Tribunal heard last year, gave the following measured assessment of religious persecution in Iran:

> In Iran all religious minorities including Christians and of course Jews, suffer varying degrees of persecution, vis a vis the Shi'ite Muslim majority. The State, since the religiously inspired revolution, does not, for example, permit non-Muslims to engage in government employment or attend university and there are restrictions on the extent to which they can fully practise their religion, for example, by teaching it. If injured or killed, they or their dependants apparently receive less compensation than would the Muslim majority, and they may suffer in assessments of their credibility as witnesses before Iranian courts.[4]

Religious persecution in Iran is a matter of public record and the subject of frequent comment from human rights observers and even from the US State Department. Louis Joinet told journalists that Iran was detaining dissidents and others without due process on a "large scale" and keeping them in solitary confinement. Human Rights Watch also reported that:

> The arbitrary detention of students and the targeting of government critics have increased. Scholars and students who criticise the ruling clerical establishment have faced death sentences, teaching bans or long prison terms.

There are many recorded cases of the execution of minority religious leaders for no other reason than that they practise their faith and organise their followers.

Iran is almost as enthusiastic as the United States in its use of the death penalty, and for much less serious offences. Amnesty records that the death penalty and various brutal forms of torture were imposed "for issues concerning freedom of association and freedom of expression". In one year alone 113 prisoners, including long-term political prisoners, were executed in Iran. Many were also flogged, frequently in public.

Although there are several Federal Court injunctions still standing between these people and other Iranian detainees threatened with deportation, it is clear that the Howard government is determined on a program of forced deportation, first of those people whose claims for asylum have failed and then of those on temporary protection visas whose countries of origin have been deemed to have improved sufficiently to allow their return. Even a cursory examination of the state of security and basic infrastructure in both Iraq and Afghanistan would lead to the inevitable conclusion that people returned would confront serious risks to their lives and health.

The government apparently wants to test the resistance of Australians to this indecency; to estimate just how profound is our indifference. I hope they are unpleasantly surprised and that Australians will draw the line at forcing people back to situations where their very lives are at risk.[5]

As I was reading the Manne and Corlett essay, I was struck by the paradox that at the same time as "a terrible coldness settled on very many Australian hearts", many others were galvanised into action as they had never been before. While the majority of our fellow citizens may have endorsed the Howard government's (and the Opposition's) "pitiless" response to those few thousand souls fleeing persecution at the hands of the Taliban and Saddam Hussein, there were many others who repudiated the rhetoric of "illegals" and "queue-jumpers" and "inappropriate behaviours". For them, *Tampa* and the Pacific Solution were a bridge too far, the moment when the politics of indifference had to be challenged.

In my nearly twenty years in public life, I have never seen so many people devote so much energy, money and time to give practical effect to their convictions: lawyers acting without fee to challenge the prolonged detention of asylum seekers; writers and journalists meticulously unpicking the contrived fabric of deceit surrounding the official policies; men and women from churches and charities raising money, collecting furniture and clothing to support the refugees refused permission to work and thrown on the mercy of the community; artists probing the impact of our cruelty on the men, women and children we sent to remote camps and refused our compassion; medical professionals insisting that we understand the inevitably destructive consequences of the policies; academics and advocates researching and devising better policies; rural Australians standing up for TPV holders and helping them endure the separation from their families; decent people everywhere writing letters and visiting those detained and lobbying politicians for their release, setting up websites and discussion groups, and writing letters to the papers and often copping abuse for their troubles; ordinary members of both the major political parties bucking their leaders and pushing for policy change.

Perhaps there is hope, after all. I know from my many conversations with these good people that they are not likely to give up until we return to a refugee policy based on the values of a common humanity. While some of us clearly want to slip into insensibility, living moment to moment in soporific detachment from the suffering of others and finding no need to puzzle over the obvious injustices in our world, others understand the need to inquire and to reach more complex understandings – and to act to reduce the suffering of others. Like Robert Manne, they are anything but indifferent.

Carmen Lawrence

1. *The New Yorker*, 17 May 2004.
2. http://www.edchange.org/multicultural/speeches/elie_wiesel_perils.html
3. Edwards, David, "Media indifference to the Afghan crisis: Why is the mainstream media ignoring the mass death of Afghan civilians?", *The Ecologist*, March 2002.
4. Federal Court of Australia, SCAT vs Minister for Immigration and Indigenous Affairs, 30 April 2002, http://www.austlii.edu.au/au/cases/cth/FCAFC/2003/80.html
5. The National Anti-Deportation Alliance has been formed to stop these forcible deportations.

Hugh Mackay

You would have to be extraordinarily hard of heart not to have wept at Robert Manne and David Corlett's account of the treatment of Shayan Badraie, for which each of us must bear our share of Australia's collective responsibility. *Sending Them Home* has done us an important service in describing, in such relentless detail, precisely how we go about responding to the plight of asylum seekers detained in our name. (This history is going to make grim reading for our children and grandchildren; they'll wonder, of course, whether we were complicit.)

Equally, having read the essay, you'd have to be soft in the head not to be puzzling – agonising – over this question: Why have Australians acquiesced so meekly in the Howard government's treatment of "fourth-wave" asylum seekers, when it stands in such stark contrast to many admirable aspects of our refugee policy? Why, indeed, are most Australians not merely acquiescent but positively supportive of the government's deliberate and systematic cruelty in relation to asylum seekers, especially children?

It is tempting to fume over the passivity of an electorate that seems to be more interested in home renovations than in the detention of children in refugee camps – or any other current-affairs issues not involving the sexual improprieties of professional footballers – but a moment's compassionate reflection might help to explain why this is so. I suspect there are at least two reasons for our silence.

First, the reality is too horrible to face, so we simply don't face it. This is a well-documented and effective psychological mechanism for the protection of our cherished beliefs. We believe that Australia stands for the "fair go", so we don't want to admit any information that might suggest otherwise. We're a harmonious, tolerant, welcoming society, so don't tell us we're not. The US military might torture its prisoners in Iraq, but we wouldn't do that sort of thing, so stories about the maltreatment of children in detention centres must either be wrong or … well, anyway, we don't want to know.

Second, Australians have been so destabilised by the experience of our very own cultural revolution – a quarter-century of relentless social, cultural, economic and technological upheaval – that we have become weary both of reform and of "issues". It's all too hard; it's all beyond our control; we feel powerless, and we don't like feeling powerless. So we disengage from "the big picture" and from the national agenda; we turn the focus inwards; we devote our attention to things we *can* control – where we'll send the kids to school, what video we'll rent tonight, where we'll spend the weekend, whether we'll renovate or move.

This is bad for the health of our democracy – partly because it lets governments get away with murder while the electorate is distracted by the choice of colour for repainting the children's bedrooms, or the need to try that new little Indian place down the street, and partly because an electorate in this kind of mood is inclined to leave it to the leader. "Howard must know something we don't know" was a common response to the mystery of why Australia found itself invading Iraq.

But it's also bad for the moral health of our society. When the focus is turned so relentlessly inward, we become more self-absorbed, more self-obsessed (which is why consumer confidence is so high) and correspondingly less compassionate, less tolerant and more inclined to let our prejudices off the leash. Who would have guessed that in the early years of the twenty-first century, Australia would be in danger of losing its hard-won reputation for tolerance and compassion towards minorities? How did this happen? To some extent, leadership is to blame. When we are officially encouraged to describe asylum seekers as "illegals", when we dehumanise people in detention centres by calling them by numbers instead of names or by degrading them in other ways, the dominoes of prejudice start to fall. If it's alright to express malevolent attitudes towards asylum seekers, why not towards Iraqis in general, or Arabs, or Afghans, or Lebanese, or Aborigines, or Muslims, or Asians?

In other words, we are having some of our darkest impulses reinforced, and this damage to the national psyche will be hard to repair. It will begin to happen when leaders – political or otherwise – begin to reinforce some of our nobler impulses by offering us a more uplifting vision of the kind of society we can become. In the meantime, it remains mysterious that a government prepared to lead the world in so many aspects of its refugee policy should be prepared to implicate us all in such a tarnished, nasty little operation on the fringes. No wonder we don't want to know.

Hugh Mackay

Anne Deveson

In the '70s, Australia moved from its grudging acceptance of post-war refugees to become a country which was beginning to grasp the concept of multiculturalism and celebrate diversity rather than shun difference. At the time I was working in various human rights areas, and I felt that we had some reason to be proud of the changes that were being made. Today, as I consider Robert Manne's devastating critique of Australia's treatment of asylum seekers, I am no longer proud. I am ashamed.

Sending Them Home is an indictment of government expediency and public indifference, which together have led to Australia having the most brutal asylum system in the Western world. It also provides a valuable historical and political perspective as part of its effort to show why and how this occurred.

When I began reading the essay, I thought that I already knew most of the background to these events. But the relentless litany of political manipulation, lies and deceit that Manne and David Corlett recount is at times almost breathtaking. They show how official propaganda grossly exaggerated the scale of the problem and consistently attempted to discredit and demonise some of the most vulnerable people in the world. The public was fed stories about illegals, queue-jumpers, opportunists, money-grubbers, people who demanded dental treatment and people who threw their children overboard. This ill-assorted rhetoric extended to people whose children drowned because an overcrowded smuggler's boat leaked, and sank. We were told they shouldn't have been there in the first place. Throughout this debate, few people protested that human rights should be accorded to everyone, irrespective of behaviour or background.

Meanwhile, in our name Australia continues to perpetuate abuses against asylum seekers that have been condemned by human rights groups around the world. The Howard government has chosen to attack or ignore these reports, just as the Bush administration initially chose to ignore reports of Iraqi prisoner abuse in American-run military jails.

I place America and Australia in deliberate proximity. Yes, the acts themselves vary in kind and in degree, but the essential nature of humiliation and degradation remains the same. Torture is torture. Brutality is brutality. In Australia, we haven't even the excuse of wanting intelligence information.

In Iraq (and almost certainly in Afghanistan and Guantánamo Bay) military prisoners are held in some of the harshest conditions imaginable. They have little access to legal representation and no knowledge when – or if – they will be released. They are beaten, dehumanised, handcuffed, shackled, held in solitary confinement, denied proper medical treatment. An unknown number have been set upon by dogs, sexually humiliated and tortured. Numbers have died.

In Australia and in the Pacific Islands, asylum seekers – whose only crime was to seek sanctuary in this country – are imprisoned in some of the harshest conditions imaginable. Manne and Corlett cite extensive testimony and research to show the extent of the damage that we are still inflicting. Here also asylum seekers have little access to legal representation, and no knowledge when – or if – they might be released. Many have been beaten, dehumanised, handcuffed, shackled, held in solitary confinement and often denied proper medical treatment. Perhaps the worst abuses are those concerning children and these are starkly documented.

In Australia, asylum seekers have not been set upon by dogs, nor is there evidence of sexual humiliation and torture. Rather than be killed, people have tended to attempt suicide. Some have succeeded in this.

One of the most damaging aspects of our present system of mandatory detention is that most people in the camps become deeply depressed and powerless, deprived of hope. *Sending Them Home* has stories of such grief and suffering among adults and children that it seems unbelievable that such misery is not only ignored, but exacerbated by a cruel and rigid insistence on never showing compassion and never yielding on draconian laws. Resilience literature concerned with psychological torture shows that while it may not be inflicted in such a dramatic fashion as physical torture, its effects can be just as devastating and last for years, sometimes forever.

The government's approach to the now well-documented increase in mental illness among those held for prolonged periods in detentions is to deny that this is a problem, or to claim that the people concerned brought it upon themselves. When John Howard was challenged about the cruelty of holding children behind the razor wire, he responded that the action of parents who bring children into dangerous situations should be the subject of criticism rather than the action of the government. He took no responsibility for their welfare.

Fear of reprisals, inside Australia and outside, prevents most people in the camps telling their stories. Yet stories are an essential part of identification and acceptance. This is what prevents the kind of dehumanisation that has led to such abuse.

> It was the muster, like animals, by number, always by number. Hen! Fox! Come here Hen 22, or Fox 30 ... and some guards are very very rude and bring the torch and shine it and wake you up. "What's your number?" And you just scared. You absolutely shocked.
>
> Two police officer grabbed my friend, grabbed his hair from the back and just bang his face to the corner of the police cage, till his face open, and blood poured out.
>
> This man from the government, he come to speak to us ... "This is not your country. This is the country of people who want to run it and rule it in this way. You are a nobody here. You have no rights."
>
> His spirit was broken, he had simply waited too long.
>
> The government started deporting people by force. They would raid the people's rooms at 4 a.m. and handcuff them. Then a few guards would hold them down and force injection into them. To make them go quietly. Someone told me the department called it "doing extractions".

These are some of the actual words of asylum seekers that were used in Ros Horin's production of *Through the Wire*, which received standing ovations during the Sydney Festival early in 2004. The play was based on interviews with asylum seekers who had fled political persecution, torture and the threat of death, hoping to find sanctuary in Australia. Instead, for three to four years they were imprisoned in desert detention centres, beaten and held in solitary confinement for months at a time. One of the young men played his own life-story in the production, while others came up on stage after the event to join the actors. Actually seeing these people who had fled such terror, and in some way or another survived, was overwhelmingly powerful.

One of the other characters in the play was Susan, a psychotherapist who had befriended one of the asylum seekers. She described her first impressions of one of the centres:

> The great rolls of razor wire were like a symbol of everything barbaric suddenly sprung up in Australia ... I had always asked myself,

how did the Germans not speak out? How did the intelligent ones not speak out? I suppose they had a death threat hanging over their heads, but we don't.

Manne tells how a "terrible coldness settled on very many Australian hearts". I wonder if this bears any relation to the terrible coldness that settles on very many of our hearts when we are asked to respect and respond to Aboriginal rights. Does it come from fear of the other, white xenophobia, arrogance, material complacency? Perhaps a mixture of all these. Are we so easily led? These are questions that need to be debated. Our present system of deterrence has worked, but at a cost which has nothing to do with the Monty Pythonesque accommodation bills that are sent to former residents of detention centres. Instead of bills, they should receive apologies. Instead of rejection they should be welcomed, in the full knowledge that people from other countries have made an immense contribution to our own.

I believe that what has happened will leave a stain on our national psyche that will not readily be expunged. Who we are and who we become is influenced by our laws, our values, our ability to connect with people from other communities and other countries, our willingness to show generosity, decency and compassion. Manne asks, "Can a political nation lose touch with moral reality?" The answer is yes. Civilisation is an ideal that can be blown away in a few seconds. At the moment, there is precious little of it around.

Anne Deveson

Linda Jaivin

In a speech in early 2004 at the Sydney Institute, Senator Amanda Vanstone pur-
ported to quote Tom Keneally, whom she accused of writing in the *Guardian* that
Australia was "xenophobic" and "opposed to entry of refugees". She stated:

> This follows a trend amongst commentators in this area. They do
> not seek to have a conversation. Your view or mine is irrelevant.
> They seek to place themselves as the arbiters of what is right and to
> lecture the rest of us on their views. They seek to denigrate the
> makers of our current border control policy. They see themselves as
> "we the righteous and principled" with the rest of us as unprin-
> cipled and ill-informed. The wide public support for our border
> control policy is nothing but an inconvenience.
>
> Such is the shallowness of much of the debate surrounding
> Australia's immigration policy.
>
> Most Australians are in no doubt that theirs is a tolerant country.
> Keneally's conga line preaches its message abroad, because they
> know it persuades no one in Australia but helpless children.

A quick check on the internet reveals that Keneally's article, "Gulags in the
sun", while replete with witty and occasionally acerbic rhetoric, does not actually contain the phrases attributed to him by Senator Vanstone. Reading the
essay, it's clear his stings are aimed at government policy and its supporters, not
country. Keneally labels compassion for the asylum seeker "the love that dare
not speak its name", and ventures that if the government continues to excise
places along our borders from the immigration zone, asylum seekers will soon
be required to reach a single table at a shopfront in Alice Springs in order to
make their claim. He observes:

Both in Australia and the UK, some would have us believe that on a slow day in some tyranny, or in a humourless and persecuting theocracy, families decide that they can have some real fun at last by abandoning houses and possessions, by hiding on trucks and trains, by marching over guarded borders, by living as an underclass in refugee camps and risking violence, disease and despair, by braving dangerous seas in questionable boats or hiding in cargo containers, all for the huge fun, the global jollity, of outraging the immigration ministers of our respective nations.

"Gulags in the sun" is available on the internet: www.guardian.co.uk/weekend /story/0,3605,1151525,00.html. The Minister's speech will be published in the next edition of *The Sydney Papers* and should appear on her own website as well (http://www.sa.liberal.org.au/vanstone). The two are worth reading and comparing.

The Minister clearly feels scorned and ridiculed by Keneally and other commentators ("Keneally's conga line"). But in lashing out against the barbs, she is only committing an act of self-harm. Her assertion that advocates don't want to have a "conversation" about the refugee issue is disingenuous, for most advocates want nothing more. Both with Senator Vanstone and her predecessor, Philip Ruddock, there have been numerous attempts at dialogue. It just doesn't work when one side won't listen to the other.

When I say "side", I don't mean "Liberals". The government's best-kept secret is the dissent within its own ranks on this issue. There are a growing number of Liberal and National MPs who are distressed by the pain and suffering this country has inflicted on thousands of innocent people in the name of "border control". They too are attempting to have a conversation with the Minister, Prime Minister and Attorney-General, the three members of the government with the most emotional investment in border-defending an ethically indefensible policy of mandatory, indefinite detention for men, women and children asylum seekers alike, and the insecure regime of "temporary protection". We can only hope these Liberals are having slightly better results than the rest of us.

If Senator Vanstone is sincere about wanting real conversation with refugee advocates in the broader community, perhaps she should start by reading Robert Manne and David Corlett's *Sending Them Home*. Without satire or sarcasm, and backed by impeccable research, the authors illustrate the impact that policy and politics and law have on real people – not just the asylum seekers, rightly the focus of the essay, but also the Australians who have become involved with them.

The essay is one of deeply felt yet calm and reasoned argument; even the most paranoid defenders of the policy would be hard-pressed to find a passage they could accuse of shallow and righteous bombast. It could be an ice-breaker; it would be nice to imagine that Senator Vanstone is capable of reading something like this with an open mind. One lives in hope.

I'm approaching my third year of visiting asylum seekers at Villawood, where I do what little I can to assist in individual cases; I've also written several essays, plays and short stories on the subject. Like many refugee advocates, I feel like Sisyphus. One asylum seeker gets his hard-won visa; another, equally deserving, faces sudden and forced deportation to a country where he is certain he will be imprisoned, tortured or killed. (And indeed, some of our deportees are now in prison in places like Iran, and some are dead.) It's a depressing, anxious world of small victories and constant crises. Perhaps some who have never experienced it first-hand will wonder if Manne and Corlett's case studies, many of which are heartbreaking, are typical; those of us who know it well can attest that they are. And the situation is a direct result of a policy that could easily be reformulated for a more humanitarian outcome.

Manne and Corlett urge the government to grant permanent residence to all temporary protection visa holders and to end the system of long-term mandatory detention. I would add two more suggestions. Most of the public discussion (including *Sending Them Home*) focuses on the Iraqis, Iranians and Afghans who make up the majority of the "fourth-wave" refugees in this country. But there is a trickle of asylum seekers who come, often by plane, from places like the Sudan, Liberia, Somalia and Sierra Leone, that is to say, some of the most dangerous places in the world, and countries that consistently make Amnesty International's "top ten" in human rights violations.

In Canada, many of these people would be accepted on the grounds that they are from a "Country of Asylum"; a class of refugees defined on the Canadian immigration department website as those "seriously and personally affected by civil war; armed conflict; or massive violations of human rights". In Australia, this is not enough. Each asylum seeker must still individually prove that he or she meets the definition of a Convention refugee – someone with a well-founded fear of persecution for reasons of race, religion, political opinion, nationality or membership in a particular social group. I would like to see us broaden our definition of refugee to encompass those from "countries of asylum". I doubt that we will, because it's just the sort of proposal that would excite visions of floodgates and hordes, but at the very least we could consider an amnesty for those in this category who have already arrived, have shown themselves to be genuine and have passed the health and security checks which are mandatory for all refugees.

The second suggestion concerns the special case of stateless Palestinian and Bedoon asylum seekers. Some Palestinians come from Gaza or the West Bank and have no automatic right of return. Others are second-generation refugees, born in refugee camps in countries like Syria, where despite noisy official declarations of Arab solidarity and pro-Palestinian rhetoric, they are treated like second-class citizens and may be readily persecuted for even peaceful political beliefs and associations.

Palestinians and Bedoons who fail in their applications for refugee status are potentially trapped inside detention indefinitely, for it is often the case that neither their country of origin nor any other country in the world wants to accept them. I know a young Bedoon man in long-term detention who told me he has now been formally rejected from dozens of countries. A landmark decision in the case of a Palestinian asylum seeker ('al Masri') last year established that in such cases, where there is no likely prospect of returning an asylum seeker to his or her country of origin in the foreseeable future, the principle of habeas corpus can be invoked. That is to say, their detention has become arbitrary and therefore contravenes the International Covenant on Civil and Political Rights.

Following the 'al Masri' decision, a handful of Palestinians, Bedoons and other stateless asylum seekers (including an Iraqi-born Hazara man) have been released from detention by the courts. But the government has decreed that they have no right to work or access any public services; their life outside is one entirely dependent on charity. This is soul-destroying and wasteful, for most of them are capable and willing to work; some are highly educated. My final addition to the suggestions made by Manne and Corlett is that these "habeas corpus refugees" be granted permanent residence and the right to work, study and access social and medical services.

Senator Vanstone – you want conversation. Could we talk?

Linda Jaivin

WHITEFELLA JUMP UP

Response to Correspondence

Germaine Greer

Too many of the people who rushed into print about my *Quarterly Essay*, *Whitefella Jump Up*, make the mistake of belittling their subject, so that one must conclude that they had nothing better to do. Some of the authors egregiously confess to being so hampered by prejudice that they couldn't address the substance of my proposition for fear that it was a "stunt". Only in Australia is my life of unremitting hard work assumed to be driven by an infantile need for attention; this libel is asserted so often that it is axiomatic and will probably feature in my obituary in the Murdoch press. I spend four months a year in Australia seeking so little attention that nobody knows I'm there, yet the sneering axiom remains unchallenged. Only in Australia is Greer "famous for being outrageous". Australian newspapers never commission me to write on any subject whatsoever, but pick and choose from what they consider the most sensational articles commissioned from me by British editors and run them under headlines that have been known to side-track a busy prime minister into condemning me for an argument I never made. This is the truth behind P.A. Durack Clancy's fantasy of my "ten out of ten for media coverage". When commonsense dictated she should have listened.

Clancy's way of defending the reputation of her Durack ancestors displays as well as I could wish just what history looks like seen from the whitefella's end of the telescope. A "well-organised, well-disciplined reconnaissance" can also be described as a "land-hungry posse"; it's all a matter of point of view. Clancy will never understand that Australia was in no need of opening up, that opening up was in fact evisceration, that what drove the operation was greed, or that the final outcome was disaster, any more than she can understand that my essay is not about her aunt who I'm sure was a wonderful person. Clancy calls me "a self-exiled academic", which will puzzle English readers who don't know that in Australia the word "academic" is an insult. Her determination to use the word is the more piquant because, though I still teach, it's more than thirty years since

I earned my living in universities. Clancy is not the only writer to dismiss me as an expatriate; Australians have still to understand that one could be a Martian and still write truth about Australia. It is a curious fact that they will accept the snap judgement of a reporter who spends two days in the country (provided it is a rave) before they will agree to consider the hard-won conclusions of someone who has spent more than half a lifetime there.

Clancy's cousin Patsy Millett, who is also involved in the Durack hagiography industry, is as convinced as she is that I wrote *Whitefella Jump Up* because I was desperate for media exposure. The sole ground for this belief is the fact that I made two appearances on Australian television in fulfilment of my obligations to the publisher of *Whitefella Jump Up*. Millett was not to know that I had repeatedly refused to perform (for a fee) for the insignificant Denton, whose impertinences I find unbearable, and only agreed to the exposure (for no fee) for *Whitefella Jump Up*, which, in keeping with his unassailable mediocrity, Denton had not bothered to read and did not discuss at all. Millett somehow managed to describe my demeanour with Denton (who was so struck by my indignation that he wrote an apology) as "mischievously flirtatious". Avid for any kind of exposure though I am said to be, I consent to my publishers' pressure to allow interviews about my work only for radio and television. So far radio and television have allowed me to give a reasonably fair representation of myself and my views, as interviews in print do not, but not to a viewer as astigmatic as Millett. She mistakes the tone of *Whitefella Jump Up*, attributing scorn where there was none, and seeing a analysis of settler mythology as a personal "denunciation" of her mother, Dame Mary Durack. Millett also states that I made "headlines" in 1972 with a condemnation of "disgusting conditions" for Aborigines in Alice Springs. I don't think of Aborigines as being kept in "conditions" like animals in a zoo, or of the Todd River camp as "disgusting" then or now. If I made any such headlines it's news to me and − as is usually the case in Australia − the words in inverted commas aren't mine. Clancy and Millett need have no fear; *Kings in Grass Castles* is still displayed in every airport bookshop in Australia and nothing I say is likely to reduce the numbers of people who just want a reasonably priced adventure story that insidiously and relentlessly displays white supremacy. The royalties will keep rolling in.

A more sophisticated version of the *argumentum ad hominem* holds that everything one writes must be about oneself, the view taken by the West Australian poet Fay Zwicky, whose poetry does seem to be all about herself, which is why I don't find it particularly interesting. So much more does Zwicky know about myself than I, I can't actually understand what she is saying. "As daughter of the priestly utterance with a vision of the ideal, her posture of defender of the dispossessed is theatrically compelling if impracticable." Cripes. I learn from her quotations of herself that Zwicky has been writing about me since 1989 and always apparently in the same patronising terms. Funnily enough for a poet, she interprets "the shortest way" as a short cut, and then intones that there are "no short cuts to anything worthwhile". You'd think, wouldn't you, that a poet would twig that the shortest way could still be very long. She should have recognised the echo of Cathy Freeman; after her win in the Sydney Olympics, with the media of the world pushing microphones and cameras into her face, Cathy said in an exhausted voice and her face stiff with a pain that was not muscular, "I just want to sit on the ground," turned away and did just that. When I say that we should sit on the ground I mean what she meant.

Les Murray is a poet of another order. I can't think why he agreed to comment on *Whitefella Jump Up*, except perhaps that he had a Germaine Greer story to tell. It is true that rather more than "a few" years ago Murray read his poems at Cambridge University and I was there. I wasn't "a lady" and I wasn't "in the back row" and I didn't assert. In fact I was rather hesitant about my question. I confessed that I had been struck by the way he read, by the liquidity of his consonants and the Aboriginality of his way of speaking, and I wondered if he would agree. He didn't reply "I've got any number of Aboriginal relatives." It wasn't such a fashionable answer in those days. He was a bit bemused by my question, as was I. There was no intention to trap him, but we have got used to Murray's irrational suspicions and I shan't take it personally. His idea that I want to transfer "nominal ownership of our country from Queen Elizabeth to the Aboriginal people" is entirely his own. The queen is not the crown; the crown is the landlord not the "owner" and the people would be us and we would have accepted our Aboriginality and we would simply claim the land for its people. Tired of me and my jejune ideas, Murray soon reverts to his own pet notion of convergence, not to be confused with assimilation, and provides a poem in support of it. We may be in the same ball park, after all, but Murray wants to own the ball.

As the latest of many white interpreters of Aboriginal society to the whites, having lived in Maningrida for a year and now writing a book about her experiences, Mary Ellen Jordan might be considered to have a better claim than most to take me to task, but not by referring to notions I do not peddle, such as "a mystical plane of higher Aboriginality". The clichés are not mine but Jordan's; because she thinks in clichés she cannot hear that I'm saying something different. Nor can she notice what I'm taking care not to say, the words

I refuse to use. She and I will always differ about the success or failure of colonisation, because she interprets the devastation she witnessed in Maningrida as evidence of colonisation, and I interpret it as evidence of its failure. America was successfully colonised; settlers spread across the country and stayed there, so that you have urban nuclei across the landmass; you have desert conurbations like Reno and Las Vegas and Los Angeles, next to which Alice Springs is a truck stop. American hunter-gatherers have enjoyed head rights, a guaranteed income without hand-outs, since the 1920s (which hasn't done them much good because like the Australian hunter-gatherers they are still in mourning for the lost land). Compared to the United States, Australia never got going.

Unable to imagine this different perspective Jordan decides that my account is "inaccurate" when my position is actually opposite to hers. Jordan frets about what my proposed "Aboriginality" might consist in, but she would have been even more fretful if I had prescribed some pseudo-Aboriginal lifestyle. Aboriginal people themselves could not describe Aboriginality, because it would be as new to them as to us. She vaguely twigs that the word would come before the fact, as a commitment, and then dismisses the idea as not new. Then she fakes obtuseness. In whose scenario would admitting that the continent is Aboriginal and adopting hunter-gatherer values involve pulling down your house and heading for the desert? It's much easier to hunt and gather by the beach, where most Australians live already. Can Jordan be the only Australian not to notice that more and more Australians are building houses in which living is done more outside than in and that our semi-naked children are out there demonstrating for sustainable development and down with the multinationals? If Australian official culture was hunter-gatherer, Australia would be committed to conservation and maintenance of resources rather than massive exploitation in the interests of RTZ and their ilk. If Australia provided the international hunter-gatherer forum, we could help to defend other hunter-gatherer minorities, all of whom are under pressure and virtually voiceless. And no, we wouldn't have to wear ochre and possum-fur.

My essay was not written for Aboriginal people or about Aboriginal people, but you won't be astonished, dear reader, if I tell you that their reactions were of overwhelming importance to me. Just as I don't know of any part of Australia that is not Aboriginal, I don't know any Aboriginal person who doesn't know (in his head) and feel (in his heart) that the whole island continent belongs to the Aboriginal peoples. It is important to me that ordinary Aboriginal people, as distinct from those Aboriginal people in charge of interpreting Aboriginality to their white counterparts, think I'm on the right track. If the central thesis of

Whitefella Jump Up is not conscientiously absurd, if the right thing might be doable after all, it is all credit to the patience of the Aboriginal peoples and none whatever to the captious and capricious whitefella. Lillian Holt's response to my groping suggestion was typically generous; she understood my silences. She saw where I couldn't go, what I wouldn't say, out of respect for the reticence of the people who've taught me the little I know. There have been other responses like hers, some from people who don't write articles for print, some from senior anthropologists who, while stroking their grey beards at my temerity, sent me papers of their own on the moral and political systems of Australia's indigenous peoples. There is a space where the idea is alive, just, but there's no hint of it on the op-ed pages of the worst English-language newspapers on earth.

Of all the responses to my essay Marcia Langton's was of the greatest importance to me. Years ago, when she was a light-hearted and astonishingly inventive activist, Professor Langton and I used to know each other rather better than we do now. Then we were friends and I thought we always would be. Now I am startled by the vein of nastiness that runs through her response; why does she think I boast about being adopted by Kulin women? What's to boast? She is perfectly entitled to doubt the "depth of my engagement in these issues" which must perforce be less than hers, but not to accuse me of "essentialist ideas about identity" as shaped by "race". The whole essay is obviously or, as Australians would say blatantly, anti-essentialist. Professor Langton calls me "Dr Greer" though I am as much a professor as she is and she knows it, and laments that I didn't address the question of Australian racism. This I didn't do because it was not my subject, just as it was not my intention to add to the volume of polemic clustering about Keith Windschuttle's amateur historiography or deplore the appalling abuse of Aboriginal women. Of course the view of history in my essay is truncated; what else could it be? Though my subject was not the suffering of Aboriginal people or the terrible offences we whitefellas have committed against them, this consciousness suffuses the whole short work, otherwise I wouldn't have argued that the wanton destruction of the continent is an expression of the whitefellas' frantic guilt. More seriously, Professor Langton makes a fundamental error in dealing with my modest proposal, in assuming that what I propose as a necessary condition for achieving any kind of cultural coherence (aka nationhood) I am also proposing as sufficient. In case I didn't make myself unmistakeably clear (and the title of the essay could mislead), let me restate it. Australia will never achieve political maturity unless and until it recognises its ineradicable Aboriginality. Ultimately Professor Langton, despite her belief that an Aboriginal Australia is a ludicrous idea, consents to move into the imaginative space of the essay. Once upon a time in the centre, she would have been less uncomfortable there.

Langton expresses regret that in illustrating two hundred years of misfit between the settlers and the land I didn't discuss more recent Australian literature, which she takes to disprove my case. Among the examples she cites is *Australian* journalist Nicolas Rothwell's *Wings of the Kitehawk*, which grew out of a commission for a series of articles retracing the steps of Leichhardt, Sturt, Strehlow and Giles. Rothwell as much as Leichhardt uses "the landscape as the sounding-board for his heart". Like Leichhardt he seeks in the kite-hawk of his title the "dark reflection of his own character". As he dashes about "discovering" a country that was never lost, he enters fully into the solipsistic world of the explorers for whom the country exists to be traversed, described, classified, and ultimately conquered. Why Langton would imagine that such a book illustrates a new relationship between whitefellas and the land I cannot imagine.

Tony Birch allowed himself to get off my case and take the idea out for a run. He has a right as an Aboriginal person to think that I romanticise settler violence, but actually it breaks my heart that people oppressed and driven from their own country ended up having to oppress and extirpate the people of another country, perpetuating the cycle of outrage in an endless proliferation of evil. It may be because I have followed the desperate struggles of my Australian forebears that I feel unable to demonise them, but he's right. I didn't. If that's romanticising their violence, I'm guilty as charged. Birch was interested and amused to wonder how my "country folk" would respond to my suggestion that they take a long hard look at themselves in the mirror and repeat, "I live in an Aboriginal country". Well, mate, I've done it. In my secret Australian life, in Queensland, echt Hanson country, I made that very suggestion to one of my workforce. "I don't consider there's any difference," he said. "I see myself as Aboriginal." I thought that was a bit steep myself, at the time, but he does work in rainforest rehabilitation, eats bush tucker in huge quantities, and treats the land with deep reverence, and I wish there were a few million more like him.

Geoff Sharp's response to *Whitefella Jump Up* is to translate my argument into his own moral terminology and to congratulate me for something I don't understand myself to have done. His attempt to argue that Australian use of alcohol is not dysfunctional is valiant, but it doesn't convince me and I doubt it would convince anyone else looking at the figures for deaths on the roads or domestic and other violence. Still, I am grateful to him because he has understood what the space is that I want Australians to jump up to, which is not mysticism (of which there is far too much already) but awareness.

It was not as if I expected readers of *Whitefella Jump Up* to bear me in triumph through the streets and cheer me to the echo. It would have been wonderful if numbers of clever people had seen some potential in my idea of Australia as an Aboriginal republic and amused themselves by seeing how far they could develop it. I cherished a faint hope that the chattering classes might kick the idea around for a week or two, long enough to see if its time might not have come, but they didn't and it hadn't. It will come though; mark my words. A hundred years from now, Australian children will be amazed to learn that Australia once considered itself a "British" country. They will understand what a hunter-gatherer republic might be, and how the interests of hunter-gatherer minorities have to be reflected in international policy because they are fundamental to any notion of sustainable development. It would make me swell in my grave with pride if Australia got to lead this international conscience-raising exercise but, as whitefellas apparently can't grasp the lesson that blackfellas never give up struggling to teach, we'll probably have to learn it from Canada and the Inuit.

I expected ridicule because, though I didn't expatiate on the vicious racism that disfigures much of Australian society, I am well aware of it. I'm used to being patronised by the stay-at-home intellectual establishment as well, but much of what was said and written was meaner-minded than would have been considered seemly in the wider world, and made me ashamed for the people who had written it. English readers will now have the opportunity to see the essay in the context of the responses that it elicited, and may come to understand why I choose to endure the manifold disadvantages and discomforts of life in England rather than return to my birthplace. And before Zwicky gets on my case again, can I just say that for me homelessness is not a disaster? For me diaspora is the true human environment and homeland a murderous delusion. I don't sing the Ha Tikva any more.

Not one of the responses to *Whitefella Jump Up* so much as gestured towards the most pressing motive for writing it, though it was plain to see. Whitefellas simply look away when I point to the devastation inflicted on the island continent in a mere two hundred years. The denial of the disaster continues; the devastation accelerates. Two weeks ago, the British invertebrate conservation charity Buglife of which I am a vice-president had to protest to the Australian government over its grant of permits for the importation of European bumble-bees to pollinate green-house crops. Just as Nicolas Rothwell couldn't see the terrible wounds on the face of the Pilbara or the exotic grasses changing the face of western Queensland, none of these commentators has understood my genuine desperation. Australia doesn't owe whitefellas (including me) a living.

They should stop ripping its guts out for a pittance, and sit on the ground. Sit on the ground, damn you, and think, think about salination, desertification, dieback, deforestation, species extinction, erosion, suburbanisation, complacency, greed and stupidity. As if.

Germaine Greer

Anne Deveson is a writer, broadcaster and documentary filmmaker. Her most recent book is *Resilience* (2003).

Germaine Greer's books include *The Female Eunuch*, *The Change*, *The Whole Woman* and *The Boy*. She is Professor of English and Comparative Studies at the University of Warwick, and appears regularly in print and other media as a broadcaster, journalist, columnist and reviewer.

Linda Jaivin is co-editor of *New Ghosts, Old Dreams: Chinese Rebel Voices* and the author of novels and non-fiction, including *Confessions of an S&M Virgin* and *The Monkey and the Dragon*.

Carmen Lawrence is the National President of the Australian Labour Party.

Hugh Mackay is a psychologist, social researcher and writer. His books include *Reinventing Australia* (1993), *The Good Listener* (1998), *Turning Points* (1999) and, most recently, *Right & Wrong: How To Decide for Yourself*.

Robert Manne is Professor of Politics at La Trobe University and a regular commentator for *The Sydney Morning Herald* and *The Age*. His books include *The Petrov Affair* (new edition, 2004) and, as editor, *Whitewash: On Keith Windschuttle's Fabrication of Aboriginal History* (2003) and *The Howard Years* (2004).

Paul McGeough is a former editor of *The Sydney Morning Herald*. He has been a reporter for almost thirty years, covering international conflict since the 1990–91 Gulf War. McGeough's work has earned Australia's highest journalistic honours, including the 2003 Walkley Award for his coverage of the Iraq War.

Amanda Vanstone is the Minister for Immigration and Multicultural and Indigenous Affairs.

QUARTERLY ESSAY

www.ingramcontent.com/pod-product-compliance
Lightning Source LLC
Chambersburg PA
CBHW080207300326
41934CB00038B/3392